THE
MEDITATION
PLAN

THE
MEDITATION
PLAN

21 keys to your inner potential

RICHARD LAWRENCE

PIATKUS

© 1999 Richard Lawrence

First published in 1999 by
Judy Piatkus (Publishers) Ltd
5 Windmill Street
London W1P 1HF

The moral rights of the author have been asserted

A catalogue record for this book is available from the British Library

ISBN 0-7499-1958-2

Text design by Paul Saunders

Typeset by Action Publishing Technology Limited, Gloucester
Printed and bound in Great Britain by
Butler & Tanner Ltd, Frome, Somerset

CONTENTS

ACKNOWLEDGEMENTS

My thanks to all those who helped me to write this book, especially the late Dr George King for his unique inspiration; to John Holder, Steve Gibson, Christopher Perry, Anthony Barnes and my wife, Alyson, for their input and advice; and to my parents, Michael and Rachel, for their unfailing support.

ACKNOWLEDGEMENTS

Introduction

'MEDITATION' IS A SIMILAR word to 'love' – it means different things to different people. To some it is a mild state of calm which helps you through life, to others it is the ultimate state of being which very few people experience in their lifetime.

To my teacher, the late Western master of yoga Dr George King, meditation was an abused word. He had entered the highest states of consciousness known in the East as 'samadhi', and could not bear the belittling of this type of elevated experience to something comparatively banal. Unfortunately for him this process has continued much further than even he expected, and meditation is now literally all things to all people.

This also has its positive side, because one thing that Dr King and others trained in the Eastern disciplines of advanced yoga always stressed was that everyone can enter these advanced states if they choose. It is not the prerogative of a select few, some spiritual élite; everyone can go there if they want to. Twentieth-century yogis such as Swami Vivekananda, Swami Sivananda and Paramahansa Yogananda all dedicated their lives to this principle, and you only have to read the works of Shakespeare, Goethe, Wordsworth and many others to see that higher states of awareness were not restricted to the East. Take this extract from Wordsworth's ode, 'Intimations of Immortality from Recollections of Early Childhood', for example:

> But for those first affections,
> Those shadowy recollections
> Which, be they what they may,
> Are yet the fountain light of all our day,
> Are yet a master light of all our seeing;
> Uphold us, cherish, and have power to make
> Our noisy years seem moments in the being
> Of the eternal Silence.

These could be the words of an Eastern mystic, but were written by someone who had no access to that area of knowledge; they were purely the result of inner realisation.

Speaking for myself, I have not yet entered the highest states of samadhi, and to be honest, it is unlikely that you have either. I have been teaching psychic and spiritual development for over 20 years, and I cannot think of a more useful yardstick than Socrates' great answer to the question designed to implicate him: Are you the wisest man in Athens? He answered truthfully that he was the wisest man because, as he put it, I know what I don't know. I cannot count the number of people I have met who, at some point in their development, overestimated their degree of personal enlightenment. They thought they were a medium for some great and vast intelligence, when in fact it was their own subconscious coming through; they thought they had experienced the ultimate state of awareness, when in fact it was no more than a positive psychic experience, they remembered a past life when they were St Joan of Arc (there must be dozens of people claiming to be reincarnations of St Joan incidentally) or some other noted figure, when in fact they may have met her or worked with her but no more. I could reel off many examples, some describing people currently on the lecture circuit, but I have no wish to be negative, only to warn about the biggest pitfall on the path: self-delusion. It is vital to know what you do not know and not delude yourself. You can then go on to greater and greater things, always grounded by your own self-knowledge.

Meditation, practised correctly, will teach you this. It will keep you grounded. It will also allow you to take off into the stratosphere in a way you never dreamt possible. The Lord Buddha taught 'the middle way' because it worked. As he taught, every imbalance in one direction has an opposite pole in the other. As dangerous as overestimating yourself is, underestimating yourself is just as limiting, and meditation is increasingly used in sport for this very reason, especially at the top levels. It is well known in competitive sport that the difference between excelling and winning is in the mind. There are many excellent sportsmen, but only a few of these become champions. Their belief in themselves and their conviction that they will succeed is absolutely crucial to achieving this status. Equally important is a degree of mental control, as can be seen from the tragic examples of sportsmen who go off the rails. Businesses are also increasingly turning to meditation-based techniques, because they know that an overstressed executive is an unreliable one. Their decision-making ability is no longer sound and eventually their whole behaviour pattern can become erratic. A few minutes of meditation every day can keep them on an even keel.

More importantly, meditation will help you to develop psychic abilities. I am amazed that other books do not refer more fully to this obvious result of correctly focused meditative practice. I can only conclude that either the authors have not taken meditation this far themselves and therefore do not know about it, or (and I hope this is not the case), they do not wish to pass their knowledge on to others. In this book I will teach you several ways of developing and using your psychic awareness. We are all different and we all develop in different ways; *Vive la différence!* as the French say. But one way or another, this system of meditation will lead on to a realisation that you do have latent psychic potential which can be used not only to help yourself, but even more importantly, to help others as well. Last year I toured Britain teaching hundreds of people how to unlock their psychic powers. I even offered a money-back guarantee (against advice from many people at the time) to anyone who did not have a psychic experience during one of my one-day workshops. Only two people asked for their money back. Most people reported several results, including outstanding demonstrations of telepathy and clairvoyance by people who had never experienced anything similar before. I was surprised and moved, and it was one of the factors that prompted me to devise the *Meditation Plan*, which, to the best of my knowledge, is a completely unique addition to the bookshelves of the world.

Another factor was the opportunity to share some of the fantastic things I have been lucky enough to experience. Not by boring you with a list of personal anecdotes, but by giving you the same keys I discovered and used along the way, so that you too can use them to make your own special journey of psychic and spiritual revelation. For example, the first time I saw a guide (someone who had physically died but still inhabits other realms of existence), it was the most natural thing in the world. They told me their name and gave me information I could not have known myself which was independently verified as being accurate. It was only afterwards that I pinched myself in disbelief when the rational left-hand side of the brain kicked in and questioned the experience. Even rationally, though I could not deny the facts. Meditation gives you the discrimination to distinguish between a genuine experience and a wandering imagination. If you had asked me when I was at university whether I would experience some of the things that have happened to me since, I would have said definitely not. If I can do these things, I know that you can too.

The first step is to know that you can achieve whatever you determine. Use this book as a manual; dip into it and choose the areas you want to work on at any particular time. Meditation can be used to improve your health, control stress, improve your sleep patterns, increase your vitality, solve problems which have been worrying you, and improve your memory. Use the keys of imagination, the 'First Eye', as a force to bring positive results in your life. We all know that if you are seeking a job and you project a positive image it will help you, both in giving confidence and in inspiring prospective employers to hire you. They are not going to believe in someone who does not believe in themselves. Controlled imagination is the secret of success in any endeavour.

Some meditation books stop there. They do not move on to the second and third steps of realisation. In traditional yoga teaching, the three stages were termed in Sanskrit: 'dharana' (concentration); 'dhyana' (meditation); and 'samadhi' (all-knowledge). Many different words have been used to describe these three stages, for example Dr King termed them concentration, contemplation and meditation. In the mystic Christian tradition on the other hand, contemplation has often been regarded as a stage above meditation. Others make little differentiation between them. Terminology is not important however, only results count in the end. As well as meditations, the book contains exercises in affirmation and visualisation. Affirmation focuses the mind on positive statements, thereby feeding the subconscious mind with the impulses it needs to operate as constructively as possible. Visualisation goes one step further by providing visual images, rather than just mental statements, which effectively create whatever goals you are seeking to bring about. Both these methods are crucial to the meditative process, and very often exercises will draw on either or both of them, as well as the more abstract form of meditation. Meditation is really a state of being, while affirmation and visualisation are methods which help to bring it about; they are all interlinked and each contributes to the others. For example, correct visualisation is one of the best ways to bring about a meditative state, while meditation will make positive thinking or affirmation more effective because the concentrative focus will be stronger and less distracted by other thoughts and feelings.

The three steps in this book are imagination, intuition and inspiration. They are the keys which will unlock your inner potential. One reason for this is that most of us are conditioned from childhood to use the deductive side of the brain, located in its left hemisphere. The right hemisphere which governs creative thinking is all too often neglected, and yet it is this which will awaken our psychic and spiritual faculties the most. The First Eye, imagination, awakens the mind and mentally creates the conditions you determine. The Second Eye, intuition, goes beyond this and starts to draw on knowledge and information which is outside of your own mind, but is in the 'mindfield' or sea of mental energy around us. It is not so much about thinking as feeling, and one of its most common features is the development of psychic abilities. With intuition you can pick up thoughts, understand other people's innermost feelings, interpret dreams, tune into the vibrations of stones and music, communicate on an inner level with animals, and even see into the future.

The Third Eye, inspiration, is the highest mental state. It is the procreator of genius, as demonstrated by those artists, musicians, scientists, orators, poets and writers who have changed the course of history as a result of inspired moments which they acted upon and turned into lasting works. With controlled inspiration, you can experience self-induced states of ecstasy, bring karmic good fortune to yourself, start to remember things about your past lives, have a natural out-of-body or astral experience, contact guides or guardian angels and enjoy true spiritual consciousness.

To move beyond that is to move into higher states of samadhi. Unlike some, I only teach what I have done myself. This is not a book of theory, it is a practical manual written by someone who has been there. If you have been there too, you might need another book – but do check with Socrates first!

A Workout for the Mind

DO YOU WORK OUT physically? If not, it would be a good thing to start doing, unless serious ill-health prevents you. A balanced regime of fitness and diet is fundamental for anyone wishing to get the most from meditation, or indeed anything else. But more important than a workout for the body is a workout for the mind. A combination of concentration, correct breathing and positive thinking will provide the best possible mental workout. These are not just things to do at specific times as exercises, but should be gradually incorporated into the whole of your life.

❧ CONCENTRATION

The brain is an organ which needs to be exercised. It is established in memory training, for example, that the biggest cause of forgetfulness is mental laziness. The greater the demand you place on the brain, the more it will respond. If you make the effort to remember things rather than looking them up or saying 'I've forgotten' and then giving up, the brain will get used to working and your memory will slowly improve.

The most effective way of working the mind is by practising concentration. This is something you can do throughout your daily life as well as during meditation practice when it is absolutely crucial. It is the ability to focus exclusively on a single thing. If you do not have this skill, no matter what psychic or spiritual abilities come to you, you will only be able to develop and appreciate them to a limited degree. You will not be able to become a reliable psychic practitioner, or control the higher states of consciousness. Nowadays, this ability is often neglected by teachers because it does not sound glamorous or appealing to most people, yet it lies at the very core of all spiritual development and at the root of all accomplishment. When focused in a positive direction, it can bring sheer exhilaration.

Meditation is a disciplined loosening of the mind, paradoxical as that may sound. You allow the mind to go where it will, and yet all the time you have complete control over the process. The faculty which provides this control is concentration. The mind wants to wander, you cannot stop it by force. Mental suppression only pushes the wandering thoughts into the subconscious from where they will bounce back uninvited until they are dealt with. So there is no point trying to prevent thoughts and feelings from occurring – instead you have to coax your mind in the direction you want it to go. You have to flow with it, using its natural attributes to bring the desired result.

➤ BREATHING THE LIFE FORCE

The 'breath of life' is not the subject of some arcane theological debate, it is a literal phenomenon. It is not just the oxygen we all need, but more importantly the life forces which flow throughout creation, and which are most readily absorbed through a correctly balanced system of breathing. I have practised yoga breathing, known in the East as 'pranayama', for over 25 years and I recommend it. There are two main things you can easily do to enhance your breathing and thereby draw into yourself the universal life force. Both are simple, but both require practice. If you practise regularly for a few minutes a day, you will find that gradually it will become automatic. Without realising it consciously you will have changed your whole breathing pattern and will be drawing in far more of the universal life force than ever before. This will bring many benefits, including increased personal magnetism and confidence, better health, greater psychic awareness and enhanced powers of concentration.

Do these exercises, and indeed all the exercises in this book unless specifically directed otherwise, seated in a hard-backed chair with the spine straight and the palms facing downwards on the knees. Avoid any type of strain or tension in your posture. If you are familiar with the postures (asanas) taught in hatha yoga and know a suitable one to use, such as padmasana (generally known as 'the lotus') or siddhasana, then that would be ideal for meditation. Although some asanas were designed for this purpose, they are not absolutely necessary – being seated with the back straight is quite sufficient.

BREATHE DEEPLY

- *Draw as much oxygen into yourself as possible on the in-breath without straining.*

- *Fill the whole of your trunk and chest on the in-breath and empty it fully on the out-breath.*

- *Draw in the diaphragm slightly on the in-breath and release it fully on the out-breath.*

• *Imagine that you are filling yourself with light from the bottom of your trunk to the top of your chest on the in-breath, and completely emptying yourself on the out-breath.*

BREATHE EVENLY

• *Make the in-breath and the out-breath as equal as possible.*

• *Get used to doing this by mentally counting so that the in-breath is the same number of counts as the out-breath.*

These two very simple guidelines of breathing as deeply and as evenly as possible without strain will change not only your breathing patterns but your mental patterns as well. You will become charged up with energy, more vital and dynamic in your approach, and yet remain balanced and in control. These results will not occur overnight, although frequently people can immediately sense the life forces they are breathing in. But they will come naturally in time. You will notice that you will start to breathe more deeply and rhythmically automatically. It will even happen in your sleep, making it deeper and more peaceful.

I must stress that these two simple breathing practices are the most elementary aspects of a far-reaching science. Yogis would use complex systems of counting different lengths of in- and out-breaths depending upon what they were trying to achieve. They would also distinguish between the effects of breathing through the left and right nostrils at specific times and even on specific days, depending upon the exact flow of life forces, which they would know precisely. One of the most elevated practices was an extremely simple one – but very difficult to perform. It was called (in Sanskrit) 'Kevala Kumbahka', and required the yogi to hold a full and deep breath in his lungs for long periods, sometimes amounting to hours. This procedure is not necessary for the practice of basic meditation, but you may find that as you develop your latent abilities you are able to hold your breath for increasingly long periods.

⤳ POSITIVE THINKING

The mind likes positive thinking; it would much rather cooperate with a positive impulse than a negative one. For one thing the positive approach is usually simpler, though not necessarily easier. If you are positive you are going in the direction you want to go in; your mental projections conform to your mental desires and that makes life simpler. Negative, pessimistic, cynical people generally reject simple solutions and are always looking for complications. Not only do they see the cup as half empty when it is half full, they expect it to become emptier. Thoughts do have an impact on conditions around us – we live in a mindfield of vibrations which are emitted in our every feeling and impulse. The chemistry between two people can be tangible because of this emission of mental energies from one to another.

A negative person pollutes the atmosphere, while a positive person heals it. A note of caution here. Some people confuse positive thinking with escapism. They use thinking positively as an excuse to avoid being realistic. Just being positive will not pay the mortgage; you also have to work for a living. Just being positive will not ensure good health; you also have to exercise and be aware of diet. But it *will* make all the difference. It is sometimes necessary to look into the abyss, to consider the worst-case scenario, and then set out to change it. What would be the inevitable result if I continued down such and such a path? The answer to that question may be negative, but it is essential to force you to change. It has certainly helped alcoholics and addicts to change when they have seen a friend die and realised it would happen to them too, unless they changed. Positive thinking is not denial. It is better to be in a real mess than in an unreal comfort zone – you then have a chance of doing something about it.

Being positive is accepting the reality of a situation, and then setting out to make it as positive as possible. If you have flu, it is no good pretending you don't. To say 'I'm well' when in fact you are ill is just to lie to yourself. Your subconscious mind will find this suggestion confusing and the end result will probably be even worse health. On the other hand, if you say 'I am getting better', the subconscious can work with this. You have not denied that you are ill, but you have decided to get better. Your subconscious receives this suggestion, acts on it and the more conviction behind it, the more you will make it happen. This is not a subtle distinction; it is the difference between success and failure.

Being positive is more than hope or even faith – it is absolute certainty. You cannot be certain about the behaviour of others, but you can be certain about yourself. Your positivity is not necessarily going to change others, in fact, using mental power to attempt to change the thinking of someone else is really a remote form of hypnotism. Be positive about yourself. Interact as positively as you can with others, but do not try to change their minds, because then you are interfering with their free will which, in my view, is a misuse of mind power. It is strange to encounter mind-body-spirit teachers who are putting out messages which border on black magic. Teaching people to use mind power to alter the opinions of others is wrong, just as it is wrong to pray that someone else changes their beliefs, as certain orthodox religions do. The magic and the prayer should be directed to send beneficial energies of good health, clarity of thought and spiritual fulfilment, not a specific belief of your own that you wish to impose. In magic, this comes under the category of performing a spell – which might surprise some churchgoers who regularly pray for their views to prevail in the world.

A fashionable view is that everyone's ideas are equally valid. We all have our own reality, so the theory goes, and no one's is better than anyone else's. If ten people perceive an object as being green and an eleventh sees it as red, who is right? A seductive argument indeed, which certainly contains a lot of truth. But whatever our individual perceptions of colour may be, and science still cannot explain what happens in the brain when we identify different colours, it does not alter the fact that the colour of an object vibrates at a fixed and specific frequency at any one time. Our perceptions of that frequency may be different, but the frequency does not change. You might think it was one frequency, and I might think it was another, but one of us is right and the other is wrong. It is a tempting philosophy to see all views as equally valid, because it enables you to accept a myriad of different perceptions without argument or dissension. But it does not help you to find the truth. If someone believes they are in contact with aliens from another planet, either they are or they are not. They may perceive that they are and that may be their reality, but it may also be completely untrue. On the other hand, and this may be more difficult for some to swallow, it may be totally and utterly true. A positive person never precludes the possibility of truth as the negative cynic does, purely on the basis of prejudice or even likelihood. The concept of electrical energy was considered extremely unlikely – and even heretical – once.

Being discriminating is not negativity. Everybody has to form judgements in life. It is a cop-out to say that you should never be judgemental about other people. The main difference between the most advanced computer and the human brain, after all, is the ability to make judgements. The most important judgements you have to make are about yourself, however. Only by recognising your limitations can you permanently discard them. People who have real self-knowledge (not false humility which is a form of ego anyway), are at peace with themselves. They are able to constructively criticise others, if necessary, without belittling them.

There are those who, far from being judgemental of others,

greatly undervalue themselves. Their self-esteem is too low. If you are one of these people, you can change; you have unlimited potential. Set yourself a realistic goal, no matter how small, and be determined to achieve it. Then go out and do it. Start with something you know you can achieve. For example, if you want to diet, start by reducing or adding a particular food. When you succeed with this, go on to the next thing, gaining confidence all the way. When you succeed with your goal, no matter what it is, be proud of yourself, pat yourself on the back, and indulge in a little self-satisfaction. As long as your objectives are sound, you will gradually build up your self-esteem.

There is too much emphasis upon difficult childhoods being the cause of all our problems. I cannot use this as an excuse since I had a superb upbringing, but for those who did not, it can be so overwhelming that they sometimes feel they will never get over it. In some cases this is understandable, but it is not helpful. It is essential to face up to the unpleasant truths about one's upbringing, but what then? A positive resolution to move on, to turn it to an advantage perhaps by helping others in a similar position. Never accept that you are and will always be a crippled member of society, that you cannot come back from it. Too many people have proved otherwise.

Life is full of opportunities to practise positive thinking – at work, at home, travelling, playing sport, going shopping, anywhere, anytime. This is one mental workout you can make permanent. At first it may be quite an effort. It requires you to change old habits. But it is the most natural thing in the world, and it will get easier and easier.

⤳ MEDITATION

Concentration, deep breathing and positive thinking are starting points for meditation, which is really a state of being rather than any specific practice. Extensive research has been

carried out into different states of consciousness by electronically measuring the frequency of the brain waves emitted by
subjects. The equipment used to make this measurement is
known as an electroencephalograph (EEG), which measures
the natural electrical energy of the nerves making up the
brain in voltage depending on the velocity of the waves.
Using this method, four main brain wave patterns have been
discovered: beta, alpha, theta and delta. Confusingly they do
not come in the correct order of the Greek alphabet. Beta
waves come at a rate of between 13 and 28 per second and are
associated with our active state of mind as we go about our
daily life, engaged in general activities. Alpha waves come at
a rate of about ten per second and are associated with a
person who may well be in a basic meditative state: relaxed,
usually with the eyes closed, but mentally focused and aware.
Theta waves come at a rate of about three to six per second
and are associated with people who are asleep and dreaming,
or in a deep, peaceful state of inner consciousness. Feats of
mind over matter have been performed in the theta state.
Finally, the delta state of below three waves per second is
only associated with deep sleep.

It is interesting that as the frequency of brain wave emissions slows from beta to alpha, the state of consciousness is
actually heightened. Other aspects of mind, beyond the
purely physical brain, will very often come into play as
distracting mental stimuli measured in brain wave patterns are
reduced. Meditation is a state of awareness, but not of active
thought. The meditator has detached from the repetitive tape
loops of thought which go round and round the brain and has
achieved a stillness of thought, measured in a reduced
frequency of brain waves. To reduce it too much leads to a
loss of consciousness and possibly sleep. Many teachers of
meditation stress the alpha state as being ideal, and it has
many proven health benefits, including decreased tension,
lower blood pressure and a stronger immune system. With
practice, you may be able to slow the brain wave patterns

even more and still remain aware and focused, in which case even higher states of meditation can be achieved. It is not necessary to know the exact rate of your brain wave emissions, but understanding the principle may help you to understand what meditation is – a reduction in mental activity leading to a deeper state of awareness of everything around you. Once you can induce this state, you are much better able to practise positive thinking, visualisation or even to awaken your psychic powers.

True meditation does not last for a few minutes, or even hours; it changes the whole of your life.

THE FIRST EYE

Keys of Imagination

KEY 1

Focusing on the Now

THERE IS ONLY ONE time – now – and we are living in it. All too often we do not realise this fact as subconscious associations constantly distract the mind. The first thing that happens when you start meditating is that a flood of thoughts and feelings enter the brain. Some of these you are conscious of and some you are not. For example, a smell of curry wafts into the room. Your subconscious associates this food with a memory, maybe of the person you were with when you last ate curry. It happens instantaneously, but at a subconscious level. All you are aware of is that suddenly you find yourself thinking about the person. Your conscious mind then connects that thought with the clothes the person was wearing, so you start thinking about clothes. This leads on to colours and so on. Multiply that with a whole bunch of other associations and connections, which are constantly going on at a conscious and subconscious level, and you can see why your mind appears to jump around like a grasshopper. In fact, being aware that the mind does jump around like a grasshopper is crucial to controlling and directing it.

The first step in all meditation is to start focusing on the now. In theory, this is impossible, because as soon as it arrives it has gone, but the very process of realising this focuses the mind. Zen Buddhists sometimes used severe methods to train their minds not to wander. For example, in some monasteries Zen masters would physically hit their students when their concentration lapsed, not as a punishment but as a discipline. Their only goal was enlightenment, and they were willing to take whatever measures were necessary to bring it about. The best form of discipline, though, is self-discipline, and to achieve this you must first become aware of your mental processes.

⮞ WATCHING THE MIND

Regard your brain as a radio receiver set, but instead of receiving radio waves through the ethers of space, it is receiving mind waves. These are translated through one of the five senses – the easiest one normally being vision. Do you know how your thinking process works? Stop reading now and try it out. Do you see pictures? Do words seem to form in your mind? Do you see words as though they were on a written page or perhaps on a screen in front of you? Do you hear sounds as though they were being spoken? Or perhaps you are aware of one of the other senses: touch, taste or smell? Imagination operates through the five senses, while feelings which you get for no apparent reason also occur initially in your imagination.

You might not have realised just how much you depend on your imagination. When you get home in the evening and decide what to eat for dinner, at some point you must imagine a particular meal. When you decide to go for a walk, at some point you have to imagine the location you are going to. Imagination operates all the time, as does memory. You never stop your mind working, you just start to bring it under control, and the only way to do this is to watch the mind and become aware of how it functions, then gradually start to guide it in the direction you want it to go. The following exercise is an excellent starting point for watching the mind.

MOVIE MEDITATION

- *Sit in a hard-backed chair and perform a few deep and even breaths with the eyes closed. Relax as much as possible.*

- *Imagine you are watching a movie screen. You are completely alone in a dark room with a large screen in front of you. All you can see is the screen.*

- *The atmosphere in the room is neutral with no distractions. Your only concern is the screen.*

- *At first the screen is blank. Relax and allow your mind to determine what appears on it. Remain alert and in control, but just watch the scene changing.*

- *If there are sounds as well as images, let them happen.*

- *If there are smells or even the sensations of taste or touch, let these happen too, as though it were a movie with some type of futuristic technology capable of producing this effect. The main thing is to allow it all to happen.*

- *If words start to form on the screen instead of pictures, let that happen too.*

- *Remain in control at all times, so that you can switch the meditation on or off at will.*

- *After a few minutes, end the visualisation of the screen completely. Return mentally to the room you are in and take a few more deep and even breaths before you finish this meditation exercise.*

The movie meditation is a way of starting to unlock your mind so that you become aware of it and of your thought processes. You will find that your mind wanders, that an issue in your life arises during the meditation which you want to think about. Instead of following this through, allow it to pass. Do not become engaged in thinking about anything in particular. You might find that for the last minute or so you have been thinking about a personal or business project and how to accomplish it. This is the left-hand side of the brain functioning, which is not the aspect of mind you want for this practice. The whole point of this exercise is that *you* determine which part of the brain you want to use. Because we are conditioned to use the left side far more than the right, it will automatically kick in, especially at first. Imagination is the prerogative of the right-hand side, and in this exercise you want to let it go where it will. You are watching it, which means that you are starting to control its function.

➤ THE FIVE SENSES

Most of the time, our senses – sight, sound, smell, touch and taste – are instinctive. They operate independently, moving from one sensation to another, registering on the mind as they do so. We are only dimly aware of how they function; it is the reactions which are impressed upon our minds. We smell flowers and then we notice they are there; we hear a dog barking and look around to see it; we see an airplane and wait for the noise; we chew on a pip and expect the bitter taste from it. These are all examples in which one sensation leads to another. This type of process can involve any or all of the five senses, but we are usually not aware of it happening until an external object brings it to our attention. Through meditation you can internalise this process. Instead of being driven by outside events, you can monitor your reactions by becoming aware of the senses. This process will introduce an element of self-control, enhance your awareness of your senses and help you to focus on the now.

CONCENTRATION ON THE FIVE SENSES

- *Sit on a hard-backed chair with the eyes closed.*

- *Breathe deeply and evenly to achieve balance.*

- *Select any of the five senses and vary this choice each time you do the meditation.*

- *Say you have chosen hearing. Start to listen to the exclusion of all the other senses. Become aware of the sounds in the room and those coming from outside the room.*

- *Stop doing this at will, and take a few more deep and even breaths.*

- *Go through as many of the senses as you have time for with a short period of deep and even breathing between each one.*

- *Sometimes it is good to do just one, sometimes two or more. If you feel that you have covered one of the senses quickly, you definitely have not covered it properly. It means you are not aware of all the sensations you are experiencing, and you need to do it again.*

- *When you choose sight, open the eyes and look ahead, absorbing all the details in your vision. You may start to see shapes changing in front of you, in which case detach from that and re-focus on what is physically there. You may also start to see outlines around objects – again detach and re-focus. These phenomena can be the beginning of clairvoyance. By detaching and re-focusing, you will develop the all-important element of self-control. If, in the future, you do start to become clairvoyant, self-control is going to be absolutely crucial. You need to determine from the beginning when you choose to exhibit your clairvoyance, and that is not the purpose of this exercise.*

- *When you choose touch, you may think there is not much to concentrate on, but you will be surprised. Become aware of each part of your anatomy and how it feels. Start from the soles of your feet and move upwards throughout the body.*

- *Smell and taste, in particular the latter, may be the most difficult. Some people have a very well-developed sense of smell, others are not so sensitive. Taste can also be developed but not during this exercise. The next time you eat, concentrate on the many flavours in the food, not because you like or dislike it, but purely to become aware of this sense.*

➥ FEELINGS

Many people believe they are at the mercy of their feelings. A bad mood comes out of the blue; a happy mood is their lucky day. Feelings are very significant, and in the Second Eye (intuition), I will examine in detail how they can lead into psychic ability. It is crucial from the beginning to set the agenda yourself, however. It is sad to meet the uncontrolled psychics, who are at the mercy of their impressions rather than using them to help themselves and others in a controlled way. As always, the main tool at your disposal to bring about this control is concentration – it will enable you to focus on the now.

CONCENTRATION ON FEELINGS

- *Be seated in the usual way with the eyes closed.*

- *Take a few deep and even breaths.*

- *Become aware of your emotional state. You may be very*

aware of it already, but focus your mind on observing how it feels.

- This may lead you to become aware of a part of your anatomy where the feeling seems to stem from. If you are nervous about something, for example, you may get butterflies in the stomach; depression can cause a sick feeling in the stomach; a passionate love can stimulate the heart, and so on. There is an inter-relationship between feelings and sensations both at a physical and psychic level.

- As you become aware of these things you may find that you gain the ability to detach yourself from emotional feelings when you choose to. This can feel strange at first, but it can be invaluable.

- You may also find that a sense of perspective comes to you. The thing you were upset about does not actually seem so bad when you observe your feelings in this way.

- If you have a tendency to overreact, this practice brings a sense of balance into your life.

- You may get feelings which lead into thoughts about imminent situations. As with the previous exercise, detach from such impressions, which can either be psychic or the result of imagination, and concentrate purely on what you are feeling now. The ability to concentrate on your determined focus to the exclusion of all else is a prerequisite of successful meditation and will pay dividends later.

➤ SEEING IT THROUGH

One of the things you will do when you learn to focus, is to see things through. This may not seem like much, but it is one of the most important qualities you possess, and can mean the difference between success and failure in any area of life. For example, most of the people who have told me that they are going to write a book one day have not done so yet; I am sure you can think of many other examples yourself. A lot of people are not even willing to see an ordinary conversation through to the end, and bring it to some kind of conclusion. It is just left as a mass of possibilities. That is fine if there are no answers, but often it is because they are not willing to exert the mental energy to try and find them.

Focusing on the now is something all geniuses have been able to do. They have been relentless in their determination to achieve whatever it is they are pursuing. It has always demanded effort and a single-minded focus, but this effort is worthwhile – and not just for the immediate results it produces. It makes life easier in the long run rather than more difficult. This is particularly noticeable among older people. Those who have exercised their brain rigorously in their life, and continue to do so when they are old, are usually far better able to cope with old age than those who are mentally lazy. The type of people who see things through are more likely to remain active in old age.

Always finish whatever you start; do not let anyone or anything put you off. This is a golden rule in all yoga and magic ritual, and, just as importantly, is a superb guide for life.

KEY 2

Better Health

MOST OF US HAVE had experience of mind over matter. In the heat of a crisis a headache has been forgotten; during an important meeting you forget you are ill; on occasions of extreme grief or joy, a minor ailment disappears, and so on. Your concentration has shifted from the focus of the discomfort or pain to other mental impulses. Sometimes it can be an effort of will, sometimes it just happens. Actors can often psyche themselves out of an illness for the duration of a performance, yet afterwards, when they have stopped acting, the pain might return with a vengeance. They can transfer their consciousness not only to a different focus, but to an entirely different personality which they have assumed in their acting role. The illness disappears as their own character is subsumed in a different one. These examples of pain disappearing, at least temporarily, when the mental focus changes, proves that the mind can and does affect your physical health.

Sick people generally turn to mind techniques for better health as a last resort, which is a shame. The mental approach to good health is one of the best preventive methods; it does not replace medicine, but can be used alongside any form of medical treatment very successfully indeed. There are outstanding cases in which patients have, with a sheer effort of will, brought about miraculous improvements. The mind is an important element which is too often ignored in medical treatments. Thankfully, doctors are increasingly recognising this fact, and in some cases will advise patients to adopt a positive approach as part of their curative process. With cancer particularly, it is now recognised that the patient's mental attitude is crucial to the healing process. For example, in Colin Rose's *Accelerated Learning* (1985), a survey was published about findings at Travis Air Force base in California. One hundred and fifty-two cancer patients at the base were rated by their doctors as to whether they had a positive or negative expectation of recovery. Without exception, the patients with positive expectations had more successful remission rates. Only two of the patients with negative expectations showed any response to treatment at all. The physician at the base stated that: 'a positive attitude towards treatment was a better predictor of treatment than was the severity of the disease'.

In his book, *Your Maximum Mind*, published in 1987, Herbert Benson M.D. referred to a study by Dr Andy T. Wielgosz and Dr JoAnne Earp of the Ottawa General Hospital Department of Medicine in Canada. They researched 106 patients, 63 women and 43 men, who had experienced pain and were attributing it to heart and coronary illness. X-rays showed that none of these patients had any significant blockages in their main coronary arteries – in fact they had a very low risk of cardiac death or nonfatal heart attack. When the patients were told this, 59 per cent still persisted in believing they had a problem with their hearts, while another 29 per cent believed they had had a heart attack in the past, though half of them admitted they had never been told that. Of the total, 23 per cent still believed they would develop heart disease in the next five to ten years. A year later the researchers again contacted the patients and found that a quarter of them were pain-free; 38 per cent had reduced pain; 30 per cent had the same amount of pain; and 7 per cent felt worse. None had experienced heart attacks. The most interesting finding came when they compared the patients' symptoms with their attitudes a year earlier. This indicated a definite relationship between their mental perceptions of their illness and the degree of pain they experienced. Those who reported no improvement were the same ones who, a year earlier, believed they would have a heart problem.

Immense research has been done and is still being carried out into exactly what consciousness is. No scientist knows exactly how the brain works or what the relationship is between the conscious and subconscious minds. Surveys such as this one from Ottawa do show that the thoughts and feelings which originate in the conscious mind, such as the idea that you have a heart problem, feed the subconscious mind with suggestions. The subconscious mind is that part of the brain which is instinctive and functional. It knows exactly how to cause the nervous system to operate in such a way that you walk, sing or jump. The conscious mind alone could not do this. It decides to walk, the subconscious mind acts on this instruction in a functional manner, and you walk. Hence the patients who believed they were likely to have heart problems passed this idea from their conscious minds to their subconscious minds, which acted on this instruction and, sure enough, they were more likely to have chest pains. On the other hand, passing a positive suggestion that they were going to get better from the conscious mind to the subconscious mind would tend to make them better. This is why positive thinking really works.

→ # TIPS FOR MINDING YOUR HEALTH

- **Thinking Health** If you constantly focus on your illness, you can reinforce it. On the other hand, if you focus on positive aspects of your health, you reinforce those. People who talk endlessly about their ailments build up a mental world of sickness which they inhabit; they are not surprised to discover yet more things wrong with them each day. If you anticipate that you will be able to go out to a particular place, for example, without giving in to forebodings of incapacity, you are more likely to do so.

- **Accepting Health** Your health is very much a product of what you do and do not accept. Many people have proved medical diagnoses wrong through pure mental attitude; a mental diagnosis gives them six months to live and they turn it around by sheer will power. This is not denial, where you refuse to even believe that you have an illness – that is foolish. You must be realistic and take the correct medical treatment. But accepting that it will never change is something else. Are you going to allow this condition to persist? Those who resign themselves to what seems to be inevitable are more likely to succumb to it than those who do not.

- **Visualising Health** Everything in life is a result of visualisation, including health. If you have a sick friend or relative, it is a good exercise to visualise them as being fit – this gives power to their recovery at a mental level. It is the same with yourself. If you are confined to bed with an illness, imagine yourself up and about doing the things you would normally be able to do, and you will help in your recovery.

- **Empowering Health** When you ask people how they are, they usually reply, 'Fine thanks, how are you?' Whether they are fine or not is beside the point; it is an automatic response to an automatic question. Most people who ask it do not expect or want any other reply, and often have not got time for it anyway as they pass you in the street or bump into you in the supermarket. This type of thing does not empower good health, it makes it meaningless. When you are healthy and someone asks you how you are, put some conviction behind your reply. It may sound like a small thing, but it is part of creating a mindfield of health around you.

- **Karma and Health** Health is a result of past thought and actions resulting in present conditions. What goes around comes around – the energy you put out is returned to you. But how you treat others is absolutely fundamental to improving your health. The more caring you are, the more you will attract care to yourself; the more you try to help others, the more help you will get when you need it. This natural law of karma has been expressed in innumerable ways in different belief systems and philosophies, but it is really very simple. You can create a karma which brings good health by serving and helping others.

➻ THE THREE-STEP TECHNIQUE FOR GOOD HEALTH

In all things, the simplest methods are often the best. No one has ever improved on water as a general, cleansing drink, only on ways of storing it, purifying it and so on. In the same way, you cannot improve upon the simplest affirmation for good health: 'I am getting better'. You can say, 'Every day in every way I am getting better and better and better', or 'I am going to get better soon', but they are only variations of the simplest of psychological tools – positive suggestion. By suggesting to your subconscious mind that you *are* getting better, you virtually instruct it to act on this information. You are in fact programming yourself to get better. The subconscious will act on this and the more force and conviction you put behind it, the more effective the results will be.

If you add to this basic ingredient of positive suggestion the faculty of imagination, you have a far more balanced and complete technique. Not only are you making a mental suggestion, you are visualising it happening, thereby activating the right-hand side of the brain as well as the left. In fact, an image of good health is far more potent than just words. Take the following sentence: I have a blue car. If you say that to someone, they may or may not remember it. If, on the other hand, you show them a picture of a car, they are far more likely to remember it. If you have no picture, but while you are talking they imagine a blue car in picture form, they will still be far more likely to remember it than from just a cold statement of fact. This is because the subconscious mind responds directly to the senses. The second essential element in any balanced mind technique is therefore the faculty of imagination.

The third vital ingredient is energy. The healing process depends upon a natural flow of energy, described in Eastern Sanskrit writings as 'prana', and by many other names in other disciplines. Martial arts practitioners were aware of this energy and used it to develop their potency as fighters; the alchemists sought it in their pursuit of the so-called philosopher's stone; and most importantly, it is the energy used by healers to bring about apparently miraculous results. To gain better health for yourself you will need to draw on this energy. The most readily available source is the air you breathe, but you can also use the power of your imagination to draw it to you.

To use these three essential elements for self-healing, practise the following exercise.

THREE STEPS TO GOOD HEALTH

- *Decide which part of your anatomy you wish to work on. For example, I will choose the left leg, but it could equally apply to any other part of you which needs healing.*

- **Step One:** *say to yourself, either silently or aloud (which can be easier for the concentration), 'My left leg is getting better and better and better'. Say this with as much conviction and belief as you can muster. Do this for a couple of minutes.*

- **Step Two:** *visualise your leg getting better. Even if it is in plaster at the time, visualise yourself without plaster, running along on it, jumping up and down and doing the type of thing you enjoy doing and would be doing if your leg was in perfect health. Do this for a couple of minutes.*

- **Step Three:** *visualise your leg in perfect condition and surrounded by a glow of shining white light, especially around any parts which have not been in good condition. Do not imagine a scene where your leg is healthy, but actually see it happening now. Start to breathe deeply and evenly, and as you do so draw a white light to yourself in your imagination. On the in-breath, draw this light into your leg as though you were breathing it in, and try to feel it. You may feel a tingling sensation or a warm heat, which are signs that you really are bringing natural energy into yourself, and this will bring great benefit to you. Do this for about five minutes.*

Although this exercise is very simple, it really does work. On one occasion I taught it during a live radio show in London. One listener who had suffered for many years from dystonia, an ailment which causes the involuntary movement of the limbs, practised it as I gave it over the airwaves. She instantly cured herself and phoned in to tell us. It must have been just the right time for her. So marked was her recovery that a doctor was brought into the same studio the following night to comment on the case. Of course you can never guarantee results like this, and you should never give sick people false hope. But the power of the mind can and sometimes does bring outstanding results. It will certainly help you to cope with illness, and even if it does not bring a complete cure, it will contribute to whatever form of medical treatment you are using.

To make it more effective still, you should try to perform this practice in a meditative state. Before starting, become watchful of your thoughts and feelings and try to induce a relaxed state of peace within yourself. A series of investigations by Dr John Kabat-Zinn at the University of Massachusetts was published in Benson's *Your Maximum Mind*. One group of patients suffering from chronic pain was treated using ordinary methods over a ten-week period. They showed no significant relief. Another group was put on a meditation program which included mental relaxation and slowing the brain waves from a beta to an alpha pattern, as referred to earlier in 'A Workout for the Mind'. The meditating group showed a reduction in pain levels of more than 33 per cent in 72 per cent of the patients, while 61 per cent of the group had a pain reduction of more than 50 per cent.

⟶ LOVE IS IN THE AIR

One of the finest callings in life is to become a healer by radiating love, as you can use this quality to make a huge difference to others. Every time you walk into a room you will affect everyone who is in it for better or for worse. The secret of healing is to bring out your own magical qualities. If you are a gentle person, this very gentleness can be used to calm and soothe those who need this energy; if you are a dynamic, vibrant personality, these qualities can charge up and revitalise all those you meet, and so on. It is not a question of trying to be someone else when you become a healer, but rather enhancing your own in-built qualities. Love really is in the air and you can radiate it wherever you go. It is not a gooey kind of sentimentality, which is only an excuse for the real thing, but a definite, vibrant, impersonal energy, which everyone can contact and channel. Take the most common form of greeting in the West: shaking hands.

SHAKING HANDS

- *Many of us shake hands with those we meet, but few of us realise that this practice is really an exchange of energy between the two people. The palms of the hands have psychic centres in them which can radiate energy, which is why the laying on of hands is used in most healing systems.*

- *Next time you shake hands with someone, imagine a light flowing down through your arm and palm and into theirs.*

- *You can enhance this, if you have time, by breathing in first, and on the out-breath sending this energy down the arm and through the palm.*

- *While you are doing this, make a definite effort to feel warmth, beneficence and love for the other person.*

- *When you start doing this, you will have to make an effort, but after a while it will happen automatically. You will radiate positive energy to others whenever you meet them and shake their hands.*

Love is the greatest healer. It is not an emotion, although it affects the emotions; it is a natural energy which flows throughout the universe. It has been referred to in many different cultures in different ways. In the Hindu scripts, the Sanskrit word prana is used to describe the natural energies out of which all matter is created. Pranayama (yoga breathing) was devised primarily to harness these energies, as yogis believed that you could breathe prana in and out like oxygen. To the Chinese it was 'vital energy'; to the Polynesians 'mana'; to alchemists 'munis' or 'magnale magnum'; and to Soviet parapsychologists, 'psychotronic energy'. It has had many names at different times and in different cultures. When you condition this natural energy with the feeling of love, it has a healing force. The greater the feeling you have for others, the more you will attract this energy to you. Some people are more naturally attuned to its vibration, but everyone can develop this capacity.

A magnetic personality is the result of harnessing this universal life force. However, magnetism of itself is not always a positive thing, as, for example, in the dynamic orations of Hitler. When you are both magnetic and condition your magnetism with a feeling of love, you will be a positive healing force wherever you go. This is not restricted to any particular type of relationship, it is an impersonal force which can be realised and felt for any human being, animal, plant or even machine. Many will attest that their car responds to the right mental approach.

One way of drawing this energy to you is to use the power of positive thinking to build an atmosphere of love in your home.

A HOUSE OF LOVE

- *When you enter your home say some form of blessing. If you do not believe in blessings, then just think benign thoughts as you walk through the door.*

- *Every so often visualise the walls, doors and windows as being filled with white light.*

- *Do the same with chairs and other furniture from time to time.*

- *Try to experience a feeling of gratitude for having your home, no matter how humble it may be. It is better to be at peace in a modest home than depressed in a luxurious mansion.*

These simple practices will help to create a positive atmosphere in your home, which will bring healing to yourself and to those who cross the threshold.

KEY 3

Controlling Stress

CONTROLLING STRESS is very different to eliminating it. We all need stress to survive, as without it there would be no motivation to do anything. The very fact that you have any responsibilities at all produces some kind of stress; a family, a job, financial responsibilities all produce stress to some degree. The pursuit of knowledge can be stressful to some people, while for others stress can be brought on by a relationship. Paradoxically enough, the absence of stress can even produce stress. Unemployed people can feel stressed by a feeling of vacancy. Lonely people can be just as stressed by their loneliness as socialites can be by their many commitments. So the elimination of stress is not only undesirable, it is futile. Those publications and courses which set as their goal a completely stress-free life are deluding the people they teach. The aim should be to have the right amount of controlled stress in your life.

⮰ UNDER PRESSURE

Whether stress is brought on by pleasure, excitement, worry, fear, or any other emotion, it can be equally challenging. It is clear that both aspects – the enjoyable and the unpleasant – are just as much forms of pressure. Some people work well under pressure, others abhor it. Pressure itself can become an addictive force in your life. For example, an undercover detective who is perpetually in fear of being discovered is under constant mental pressure; a top politician whose illicit, secret behaviour would destroy his career, and possibly his marriage, is also under intense pressure. In both cases, the element of danger can become addictive. It causes an adrenaline rush, which they thrive on. When these situations come to an end through retirement or another cause, the danger is removed from their life and with it goes the adrenaline rush which they have become used to. It can be like coming off drugs, and some find it very difficult to adjust to a 'normal' life. But there is a major difference between these two cases, namely the motive. The undercover detective is adopting a lifestyle because he believes he is performing a service to the community; the politician has a problem of his own making. The politician can alter the situation by self-control; the undercover detective is having to deal with conditions beyond his control. If the politician was capable of meditation, and in a truly civilised world I believe he would be, he could bring about the internal changes necessary to control the forces at work in his life.

In examining the pressures in your life, this is the first judgement you have to make. Can I do anything about this situation? Are these forces beyond my control? If they are, you need to practise the meditation of acceptance. What you cannot alter, you must accept. By not accepting the inevitable you are fighting a pointless battle, which is detrimental to you both psychologically and physically. Many people do just that; they spend much of their life railing against hopeless situations, thereby draining themselves of energy and achieving nothing but further anxiety. Life can seem very unjust, but it has to be adapted to. This does not mean that you should give up fighting for a noble cause, providing you have a chance of doing something about it. But no responsible general would lead his troops to certain death just on the basis that the other army was being unfair to them. He would accept the impossibility of the present battle conditions and live to fight another day.

➤ KARMA

The single most helpful philosophy in coping with this type of outside pressure is a belief in karma. Strangely, karma has become a trendy word nowadays, though it is one of the oldest on earth. When its true meaning is accepted and it still remains trendy, the new age will really have arrived!

Karma means give and take. As you sow so shall you reap (the Bible); to every action there is an equal and opposite reaction (Buddhist scripts); you get what you create (common sense). It means that serving others is one of the finest ways to help yourself. Every time you share knowledge with others, you are that much more likely to receive knowledge yourself. Every time you help a person, animal or even plant, you are that much more likely to receive help. You should not perform an action for that reason, however, or it won't work, because your motive would be selfish and it would not really be a service at all. Freely giving to others is a path to freedom for yourself.

There are those cases which seem desperately unfair – how could anyone deserve to be born in a hopeless, suffering situation? They have never harmed anyone, they are an innocent baby. This is the most difficult question of all to answer. Orthodox Christianity fails this test abysmally. The doctrine of original sin (that in some way we are sinners before we are even born) is far too wishy-washy to deal with this crucial question. It can only be explained by a belief in reincarnation. Karma without reincarnation is like the universe without planets; it is a framework for evolution without the evolving souls. A single lifetime is not sufficient for a soul to manifest their full potential by any stretch of the imagination. This does not mean that everyone who is born into a difficult situation behaved wrongly in their past life. We have all had countless lives; the karma of this life may be the result of our actions a very long time ago. But the purpose of it all is to *learn* not to punish or reward. Some lives will be far easier than others for all of us. When you find yourself subject to stressful pressures which are outside your control, a belief in karma and reincarnation will help you to accept the situation and not constantly fight an impossible battle. Those who think they are badly done by, especially if they become bitter, damage their health and their psychological outlook as well as their karma.

➣ TRANSMUTATION

Accepting conditions is only the first step, removing the internal pressures brought on by annoyance, justification and self-pity. You then have to transmute the problem and regain control over your stress levels. The following exercise will enable you to do this.

LIGHTEN THE PRESSURE

- *Breathe deeply and evenly a few times.*
- *Become aware of the points of mental tension which are causing stress. Do not try to solve them in your mind or even think about them. Just identify the issues in your life which are pressurising you. If you are not sure exactly what the problem is, vaguely identify possible areas.*

- *Regard these as you might points of tension (pressure points) in the physical body; they need to be massaged out. Rather than using the fingertips to do this, you will be applying light through visualisation.*

- *Identify an issue (pressure point). As you breathe in, imagine you are drawing light into that issue. See it illuminating your whole being – body and mind.*

- *On the out-breath, release the issue, again bathed in light. Do not imagine your problem being breathed out of your system, as some teach. Thoughts are things, and by releasing negativity you are inflicting your problems and tensions on the mindfield around you, which will affect others and eventually rebound on yourself. Always see your mental tensions being first transmuted in light and then leaving you.*

❧ SHIFTING PARADIGMS

We all build up paradigms or patterns of behaviour and thought. These can be repetitive, like tape loops, going round and round and returning to us until we break them and shift into another paradigm. This is not always easy to do at a deep level. You can go through the motions on the surface, but it will not last unless you make a genuine, inner change. For example, you may think you have been wronged at work. You believe someone has told lies about you in order to advance their position, and as a result they have been promoted instead of you. This type of thing can gnaw away at you and go round and round in your mind. First you need to see if there is anything you can do about it that you have not already tried. If you know there is nothing further you can do, there comes a point at which you need to detach. Nothing useful is gained by going over and over an incident in your mind. Meditation provides the key to this detachment. It takes you into another state of consciousness where things take on a different perspective, and you can move on. This is very different from suppression, which only leads to further bitterness in the end. It is a release from a mental pattern, however justified it may be, which is of no productive use to you.

SURFING THE MIND

- *If you are computer-literate you will know what it means to surf the web. You move from one site to another, each one connected to many others by common topics. Surfing is moving through these inter-connections and seeing where it leads. You can do this with the mind.*

- *If you have a paradigm of mental behaviour going on in your head like a tape loop, you can release it by following its inter-connections. One thought will lead to another in a random manner.*

- *Let this happen without trying to work out or calculate where it is all going or why.*

- *See where you end up. Even if this exercise appears to go nowhere, just by attempting it you are starting to shift paradigms. The subconscious mind will begin to realise that you want your mind to move on, and gradually, with practice, you will ease yourself out of one mind set and into another.*

How do you sleep at night? The very question suggests a troubled conscience preventing a good night's sleep, which means that at least you are aware of your conscience. But many things, including physical disorders, diet, and so on, can cause insomnia. Advanced yogis were able to induce a state of such complete relaxation at a physical, mental and emotional level, that they could get the equivalent of a good night's sleep in just a couple of hours. The thing to avoid is a vicious circle of not sleeping and then worrying that you are not sleeping, which itself causes you not to sleep, and so on. You can do this simply by letting go. Do not worry whether you are sleeping, but do not give up either by getting up and eating or reading. Every time you do this you signal to your subconscious mind that it rules the roost. By lying there and not sleeping but at least relaxing you are informing the subconscious that you have decided to sleep at this time and, providing you need it, you are more likely to do so. This approach will gradually help you to overcome insomnia.

Sometimes you are not sleeping because the mind has matters to attend to which require you to think. In this case you can lie in bed and surf the mind. Avoid thinking consciously about a specific problem, but let it wander. The mind does not switch on and off, it just shifts from one paradigm to another.

⟩ SERVICE TO OTHERS

Service is often seen as a thing of duty when it should be a thing of love; it is not something you do because you *ought* to, but because you *want* to. It may surprise you that serving others actually relieves and controls undue stress. There is too much emphasis in psychological teaching methods on subconscious tensions, and not enough on superconscious ones. The superconscious is the highest aspect of mind, which includes the conscience. Guilt of all kinds is frowned upon nowadays; it is not politically correct to feel guilty about anything. Yet the old-fashioned pricking of the conscience causes us to help others when we do not feel like it, to contribute to charity and so on. When you turn the natural impulse of conscience into a whole-hearted desire to serve, you automatically transmute many in-built tensions. By concentrating on the problems of others, your own problems diminish and fall into perspective. Having an extension built on to a four-bedroom house can bring anxieties, but nothing compared to the anxieties of having nowhere at all to live.

Just reminding yourself of things like this brings a sense of gratitude for what you have, which removes stress.

Apart from the death of a loved one, moving house is considered the most stressful thing we can do in the modern world. It would be the threat of war in the Middle East or starvation in Rwanda if we were more civilised. One of the reasons for being self-centred is the belief that you really cannot do much to help others anyway. This is completely wrong. Just as you can heal yourself, you can also heal others. The following exercise is best done after you have achieved a meditative state and are therefore able to focus your mind on channelling healing energies, without any conflicting thoughts getting in the way.

HEALING OTHERS

- *Raise your hands so that the palms are facing outwards.*

- *Visualise the person or situation you want to heal as being bathed in light.*

- *If there is sickness, conflict or negativity of any kind in the situation or person you have chosen to focus upon, mentally turn this into a positive situation of good health, harmony and peace.*

- *If you are religious, you may wish to say a prayer at this point for a positive outcome to the situation you have chosen.*

- *Remember not to try to change the viewpoint of anyone involved, only to send them light and bring as positive an outcome as possible.*

The next time you are watching the news on television and you see reports of famine, warfare and so on, turn off the television and do the above exercise. It is no good feeling helpless and depressed about a world situation; if everyone were to send out positive mental energy in this way, it would change the world overnight. Your efforts may bring far more good than you think. Prayer and healing have been proved statistically to work. In 1988, Dr Randolph Byrd, a prominent cardiologist, conducted a fascinating study. A computer assigned 393 patients at the coronary-care unit of San Francisco General Hospital either to a group that was prayed for or a group that was not. The prayer groups were given patients' first names along with brief descriptions of their medical problems. They prayed each day until the patient was discharged. When the study was completed ten months later, the prayed-for patients were five times less likely to require antibiotics, 2.5 times less likely to suffer congestive heart failure, and less prone to cardiac arrest. Dr William Nolen, who had written a book questioning faith healing, stated: 'If this is a valid study, we doctors ought to be writing on our order sheets, "Pray three times a day". If it works, it works!'

With a simple exercise like this you can do fantastic good for others. In doing so, you will also remove a blockage from your subconscious, which is unsatisfied by an existence focused solely on yourself and those you love. Despite the enticements of money, sex and fame, which are constantly bombarding us through advertising and the media, there are numerous cases that prove that none of these things can be guaranteed to 'hit the spot'. Our lives exist in a whole – we are not a haphazard bunch of isolated units. Without service to others, there will always be something missing; with it comes lasting fulfilment.

KEY 4

Staying Young

YOU ARE AS OLD as you feel. That is all very well when you are fit, but how easy is it to feel young when your body starts to deteriorate with old age? There are some remarkable examples of people who have proved that they are still young in their eighties and nineties. It is all to do with mental attitude. Old age is an infirmity of sorts, a kind of disability. Maybe you or someone you know is disabled; you will therefore know what disabled people can and have achieved with the right attitude. They will tell you that the attitude of others to their disability is crucial as well. They do not want to be humoured or patronised, they want to be given a chance to prove that they are just as capable of doing most things as anybody else – more capable than many who are not disabled. The same is true of old age.

❧ STEP ONE: NEVER GIVE UP

It must be so tempting to give up sometimes. You know that

society at large will completely understand, as will your loved ones and friends. I have elderly parents and many elderly friends, and those who remain mentally active are also the most physically active. The very idea of retirement is destructive to them. I do not necessarily mean retirement from a particular job, but retirement from being active; giving up because you have reached a certain age and are therefore a 'retired person', who has no active role except maybe looking after the grandchildren from time to time.

The final stage of your life can be the most valuable. It is not an aftermath to the main event, but an opportunity to use the experiences of a lifetime in preparation for the next one. Reincarnationists like myself have a very different view of old age from those who do not believe in life after death, or who just have a vague idea of passing into some perpetual heaven where grapes and harps are common features. Incidentally, this concept of heaven is a place where most people would be excruciatingly bored (what would they do without television?). But if you believe, as I do, that one life is just a flash in the pan, then the period before passing onwards must be the most important time of all. It is the time when you prepare for what is to come next – the exact opposite to giving up. The Egyptians understood this well as can be seen from the inscriptions on their tombs and burial sites, which comprise *The Egyptian Book of the Dead*. The Tibetans, too, in *The Tibetan Book of the Dead* give detailed instructions on how to prepare for passing. The frame of mind in which you spend your last years is all-important.

But there is far more to old age than preparing for death and the next life. It can be a very productive period, when you are free of some of the mundane responsibilities which distract the mind. Many Hindus consider it to be a sublime period for meditation and reflection on higher things. Uncluttered by worldly ambitions and commitments of various kinds, the mind can soar and remain active, while being focused on ethereal matters. Lack of time is the reason many people give for not pondering the reason we are on earth. It would be far better to alter one's priorities earlier in life, but certainly, in old age, we are meant to devote time to reflection on our purpose for being here. Rather than being an epilogue to a material existence, old age is an interlude in a spiritual one.

➤ STEP TWO: INCREASING YOUR VITALITY

We live in a sea of magnetic energies. Being a magnetic personality is not something that just happens to you – you can make it happen. Nor is it related to age – a young person can be dull and listless, while an older one can be vibrant and leave an impact wherever they go. The natural life forces pervade the universe and are readily available. According to Eastern writings, they are assimilated through our psychic centres or chakras. Sanskrit texts speak of no less than 72,000 channels, called 'nadis', inter-connecting through the ethers within and around our bodies and channelling these energies in one form or another through each one of us. The subtle body around the physical body, the aura, is composed of etheric matter, known in Sanskrit as 'Akasha'. As well as the inter-connecting nadis, which operate like a subtle version of the nervous system, sending energetic signals throughout the aura, we have subtle nerve centres, the chakras. Of these, the seven most important ones are, in ascending order: the base of the spine centre; the sex centre; the solar plexus or navel centre; the heart centre (which is central, not on the left like the physical heart); the throat centre; the Christ centre or third eye, which is between the eyebrows; and the crown centre above the head, from which the halo is taken. The centre which will most increase basic vitality is the solar plexus centre. Based on this principle, the following is an excellent technique for drawing magnetic energies to yourself.

BATTERY CHARGER

- *The solar plexus is the psychic centre which acts virtually as a human battery. By charging and re-charging it you can revitalise yourself with magnetic energies.*

- *Place your right hand just above the navel, covering the solar plexus.*

- *Place your left hand on top of the right.*

- *Breathe as deeply as you can. On the in-breath, visualise white light entering the whole of you.*

- *On the out-breath, visualise this light travelling down the arms, through the palms of the hands and into your solar plexus.*

- *You may feel one or more of the following: heat in the palms of your hands or solar plexus; pressure on top of the head; a general tingling throughout your body. These are all signs that the practice is working and you are re-charging yourself.*

- *Do this for a few minutes whenever you feel depleted.*

Another method of re-charging your batteries is through correct relaxation. Tension can block the flow of mental energy and it is a very good idea to completely relax yourself from time to time.

TOTAL RELAXATION

- *Put a blue light bulb in your light, table lamp or standard lamp. Only use this light. Blue is a cold, relaxing colour, particularly beneficial for those who suffer from nervous tension or are mentally hyper-active.*

- *Lie on your back on your bed or the floor.*

- Bit by bit, mentally go through every part of your anatomy, instructing it to relax. Only when it does so, move on to the next. Do this gently but firmly.

- Mentally pull the blue light into you and imagine you are floating on your back in a calm, still ocean of blue light.

- Allow the blue light not just to surround you, but try to see and feel it going through your body as though you were only an outer shell and inside you was just this pure, blue energy.

- Bring yourself mentally back to the bed or floor.

If you do this from time to time, you will find it easier to charge yourself up magnetically when you want to. It would be a very good thing, after doing this exercise, to sit up and practise some deep and even breathing, drawing white light into you as you do so. You will find that you are more receptive to the natural life forces readily available in the air that you breathe if you are totally relaxed first. Like a magnet attracting metal, you will draw the universal life forces into you and thereby increase your vitality immensely.

❧ STEP THREE: OLDER AND WISER

It is not strictly true to say that an older person is necessarily a wiser one. For one thing, they may have learnt very little in their lifetime, for another, one lifetime is a drop in the ocean. Someone who is physically much younger in this life may be an older soul than the older person. However, the older person should know the ways of this world better, having spent a lifetime in it, while the younger person, no matter how advanced they are, has not been physically alive for so long. By the same token, young people do not have a monopoly on enthusiasm and concern for humanity. It is very often middle-aged people who get burdened down by responsibilities and lose sight of the big picture, while they focus on paying the bills, looking after their family and maintaining their job. But this is not necessary either. Middle-age could be the most productive period of all, when you pretty much know what you are cut out for, and it is not too late to go for it.

It is all a question of mental outlook. To follow are some pointers to look out for so that you can make sure that as you get older you also become wiser and not vice versa. Think about the points, and then meditate upon them in turn by leaving your mind open to the many other aspects of each one which come to you. By meditating on them, rather than just thinking about them, a fertilisation process takes place within you which will bring a deeper, more natural realisation, rather than just an intellectual appreciation. You can then go one step further by seeing yourself in various situations in life, demonstrating these positive qualities.

- **Avoid cynicism** It is a destructive force. It may be amusing, but slowly it undermines the fabric of your thought patterns and you start to take a twisted view of life, of the people you meet and the situations you find yourself in. It inevitably leads to a pessimistic view of life. Of course, it is no good being naive, but there is a big leap between naivety and cynicism. Be realistic about life, but never cynical.

- **Cultivate optimism** It is the perfect antidote for cynicism. Not the kind of optimism which is based on fantasy and therefore leads to disappointment, but the kind of optimism which always focuses on the most positive possible outcome of a situation while keeping your feet firmly on the ground. It is a positive energy which will influence events for the better.

- **Keep the faith** It is something we all need. It is very easy to become a distrustful person when you have been let down a few times, but as you get older you should never lose the ability to trust, not out of blind faith, but because you know and appreciate the value of it. Of course there are limits; you need to be prudent in your financial affairs and so on. But if you lose the element of trust completely you will attract distrust from others and create a vicious circle which is hard to get out of.

- **Reject unhealthy scepticism** Of course there is a place for healthy scepticism, but it can go too far. If your first tendency on hearing the unusual is to doubt it, then you have become a conditioned person. All the great scientific inventions, new philosophies and artistic movements were unusual when they started, yet many of them later became orthodox. There is absolutely no reason why an unusual thing is less likely to be true than something you are used to. Adopting this attitude will definitely help you to stay young.

- **'Can do' approach** If your first instinct on being asked something is to say, 'I don't know', and then to think about it, you are slipping into a 'can't do' approach. If your initial impulse is to evade situations, avoid responsibilities and not get to the bottom of problems, you are on a slippery slope. A 'can do' approach is not just something for management consultants in business seminars, it applies across life. By having this approach you stay involved; you are not past it, you are a player. In fact, young people can be far less 'can do' than older people.

Wisdom is not about spouting platitudes to fit all occasions, it is an energy which others feed off. There is nothing more inspiring than an older person who has not given into their years. Most of all, they are still learning. The wise person is not the one who thinks they have arrived, that they know more than everyone else because they have lived longer; they are a person like Socrates. In order to know what they do not know, they have to stay young.

KEY 5

Improving Your Memory

MEMORY IS OFTEN misunderstood. Some people think you either have it or you do not, that you have no control over the situation at all – you are either blessed with a good or a bad memory. The first thing to do if you want to improve your memory is to stop saying, 'I can't reme~mber'. Whenever you say that you are feeding your subconscious mind with the instruction that it is incapable of remembering and it will act accordingly. The one sure way to make your memory worse is to constantly say that you have forgotten things. Instead, you need to acknowledge that everything you have ever learnt is stored in the most brilliant, computerised filing system you will ever come into contact with, namely your own subconscious mind.

❧ MEMORY IMAGING

Visual images are generally the easiest things to remember. Most memory systems are therefore based on a carefully devised series of visualisations connected to the thing you are trying to remember. Experts realise that the faculty of imagination is absolutely crucial to this process – it is not just a case of coldly trying to remember facts, but of programming the mind with definite images which themselves will trigger responses. Methods of speed-reading have been devised through which experts can memorise the salient points of books while spending just a few seconds on each page. They avoid the lengthy procedure of intellectually digesting and comprehending the written words, and instead memorise the shape and structure of the words on the pages. Through this visual process, they assimilate the information there without having to consciously think about it. The programming part of the memory process is done without any rationalisation or understanding of the material whatsoever – only the ability to absorb it. Later, when trying to recall the pages of the book, they start to consciously realise what they have memorised. Using this method, outstanding demonstrations have been performed by experts in which whole chapters of books have been read in a matter of seconds. When questioned about them later, the experts have accurately described their content.

Other memory techniques involve using the most potent visualisations possible to aid the self-programming process. These visualisations are often of a bizarre or violent nature because shock images are easier to recall. For example, Mr Rodney Appleby might be visualised with a face like an apple and a rod sticking through his knee. Absurd as this sounds, you will never forget his name again. You will not always remember the visualisation – that was just used for the programming phase – but you will remember his name when you see him next. Techniques like this are taught in business training programmes to help remember colleagues and customers. They are also used to help remember facts for passing exams, even though they throw no real light on the intelligence of the student.

This principle (known as mnemonics) is also used to

remember numbers, which are first reduced to letters and then turned into words which become visual images. Codes have been devised which immediately convert a number into a letter of the alphabet. As you hear a number you instantly think of it as a group of letters – a word. This may sound complicated, but it enables financial speculators, for example, to 'see' a number rather than think it, which, in turn, helps them to remember a multi-digit number instantly. In certain lines of work this is not only impressive, but also extremely useful.

With practice, the process starts to take place automatically at a subconscious level. Professional entertainers have used it to memorise an audience of 200 strangers and repeat their names back person by person an hour later.

As impressive as this is, how beneficial is it really? It is a short cut which gives you short-term memory, but at a price. It enables you to quickly assimilate information and remember it for a period of time afterwards. It also exercises the brain and therefore improves your thinking process. It does not, however, necessarily lead to improvement of your long-term memory. And there is another downside to it. The bizarre and violent images will have an effect both on Rodney Appleby and later on yourself, since what you send out is returned to you. Also, these methods of memorising facts, bypassing the conscious mind as they do, remove the element of discrimination. You could be programming yourself with all sorts of incorrect information, and have not given yourself the opportunity to think about the information before storing it in your in-built filing system. You are, in fact, literally brainwashing yourself. It is superb to watch world experts performing the feat of reading page after page of a book at lightning speed, and then being able to recall the information they have absorbed. But it also means that they have planted in the recesses of their minds, indiscriminately as fact, whatever is in the book they have read. They have not given themselves the opportunity to decide what they believe first, and this will affect their thought processes at a subconscious level for better or worse. It is like allowing yourself to be hypnotised by the author, instead of reading what he has to say and forming your own views on it – and that is a very exact parallel. Hypnotism is allowing the hypnotist to control your thought process and plant new thoughts into your mind.

Many thousands of years ago the ancient Hindus wrote of a time when the written word was unnecessary. Their ancestors had been able to memorise thousands of stanzas of religious verse purely on being told it orally. They must have entered some form of trance in which they were able to bypass their conscious processes and immediately absorb the information at a subconscious level. Once absorbed it was there for them to gradually assimilate, comprehend and apply in their lives. They were willing to take this on faith as an initiation because they had such respect for their teachers, who were known as the Rishis. It would take them some time, possibly many years, to realise the full meaning of what they had learnt. The Rishis, for their part, were very careful whom they imparted such information to, to ensure they were ready to receive such wisdom.

This type of exceptional ability, which is also reputed to have existed in ancient Egypt, has long been lost. And even if we had it, it is still no substitute for a conscious faculty of memory which, though slower, does not depend on any form of trance, violent or bizarre imagery, or the assimilation of material without any discrimination whatsoever.

➤ NATURAL MEMORY

It may be slower, but there are many advantages in improving your memory naturally, without using a short cut. The most important advantage is that you will find that your memory starts to co-operate with you, not only when you want it to, but all the time. For example, if you use a system involving extreme imagery to remember names, it will work. You will remember people when you see them, but the subconscious will start to expect this type of programming method. If you use the basic principles of visualisation, i.e. consciously giving yourself a picture of the person rather than just a name, but one which is not a distortion of nature, you are more likely to remember it. For example, in trying to remember Rodney Appleby, you visualise a picture of the person with a rod on their knee (rather than through it) and an apple in their hand. It may be slower, but it is a completely natural image. What may then happen is that, at an appropriate time, because your image has conformed to nature and has been benign rather than violent, their name will pop into your head when you are not trying specifically to remember it. It may be that you have an appointment to see the person. You are not sitting there consciously trying to remember them, but they just pop into your head at the right moment so that you do not forget your appointment. I call this *natural memory*. It is slower in the initial stages, but is far more useful in the long term. It is the difference between developing a short-term memory when you *want* to, and the natural ability to remember things when you really *need* to.

So-called 'false memory syndrome' proves that it is possible to confuse fantasy with reality. People who suffer from this genuinely believe that things have happened to them which have not happened at all. Perhaps their fears were so strong that they lost the ability to discriminate between what they dreaded and what really happened. This is most acute in certain cases involving children, who have very vivid imaginations and sometimes, though not always, report harrowing scenes of abuse and so forth, which they really believe happened but are later found not to be based on fact. It can also apply in more minor ways. There are numerous incidents, witnessed by several people, which are remembered very differently indeed depending on the perspective of the person involved. Their particular slant or emotional involvement causes them to imagine aspects which never actually took place. Hence the need to always remain vigilant in the controlled use of the imagination in memory techniques.

Neuro-linguistic programming, which has become very popular and really does work, also fails the natural memory test. The theory is sound and has been developed by, among others, hypnotists. It teaches you to identify particular thoughts and feelings with physical sensations – you programme yourself by remembering and visualising a time of great joy and then, while you are doing this, performing a physical action such as touching your leg with your hand. This identifies, neuro-linguistically, the feeling of great joy with the physical action. Later, at a time of depression, say, you are able to recall the joyous feeling by touching your leg with your hand. So far so good. It can be used to give you confidence and all sorts of other qualities virtually on demand. The only problem might be that the depression is telling you something. You have blocked it out but you have not removed the reason for its existence. It is a superficial process, which may help you on many occasions, but it does not fall into the category of natural memory. Like hypnotism, it might be extremely helpful, particularly relating to health, but to develop a long-term memory, which operates not just when you want to artificially change your mood or emotions at will but brings a lasting, internal change for the better, I would recommend these natural memory guidelines.

- When you want to remember something or someone, visualise it or them in picture form as vividly as possible.

- In forming this picture allow these two guidelines: make sure it is a positive image; make it as true to life as possible. See the object or person in a natural situation which could really exist, and which is completely benign.

- Learn to do this as speedily as possible so that it becomes instantaneous.

- If there are numbers or dates involved, see them as figures in your picture. If particular numbers have particular meanings to you, you can devise a visual code so that each number is represented by an image.

- If there are names involved, see these as images in your picture as well.

- In this way you will turn words into pictures in your mind, but you will not introduce negative elements into your visualisation process.

MEMORY MEDITATION

- *Pick an event you wish to remember. It may be the performance of a play; a book you read a year ago; the events of last Saturday; anything you choose. As you get better, you will be able to pick more difficult subjects.*

- *Start by going over in your mind what you consciously remember about the subject you have chosen.*

- *As you do this, maintain a regular pattern of deep breathing and start to loosen up your mental processes by allowing memories to come to you, rather than trying to force them.*

- *Stop consciously going over the details, but just allow images, thoughts and feelings to float into your mind. If your mind starts to wander off the subject, bring it back to the main focus, and then let it float randomly again.*

- *With practice, details will start to come to you about the subject which you may not have noticed very clearly when they happened, but which were stored in your subconscious mind.*

This meditation uses the principle of activating the imagination to enhance the memory process. It is slower in the early stages than the indiscriminate method, but it will be far better for you in the long term. Thoughts are things, and all your visualisations have an effect on the ethers around you. If you create bizarre and negative images, they will sooner or later start to affect the way you think about everything. We are a reflection of our thoughts; someone who holds benign and positive thoughts not only co-operates better with the natural process of their subconscious mind but also, and even more importantly, co-operates better with the natural karmic law of cause and effect. What you put out is returned to you, so it is in your interests to make sure it is always as positive as possible.

KEY 6

Solving Problems

O N 10 NOVEMBER, 1619, in the small Bavarian
village of Ulm, René Descartes had a dream in
which he saw a method by which all human
problems, whether of science, law or politics, could be solved.
This was to be the method of reason. All knowledge, according
to his dream, could be discovered by systematic, logical
computation. But then he was the man who said 'I think therefore I am' instead of 'I am therefore I think' (which is an
aphorism in yoga philosophy). As valuable as inductive reason-
ing is, and Descartes was unquestionably a master of it, it is not
complete without the faculty of imagination.

❧ ALTERING YOUR MIND SET

There are famous examples of the answers to problems just
popping into the head, rather than being the result of logical
deduction. Einstein hit upon the theory of relativity while
daydreaming about the moon; Archimedes was in the bath

when he suddenly realised how to measure mass; writers and composers would sometimes come up with their greatest works in a sudden flash. They may have spent many hours thinking about it, then they let their mind go in a daydream or by relaxing, and suddenly what they were looking for came to them. The secret is getting the mind into the right state rather than exerting mental effort on the problem itself.

A teacher of scriptwriters gave a good example of this. He had a pupil who was asked to write a script for a thriller, but suffered from 'writer's block'. Nothing would come to him; he dried up as soon as he started to think about the task, a frightening state for any writer to be in. The teacher discussed the problem with him and asked what he really wanted to do. He said he had always wanted to write a comedy. The teacher told him to go ahead, forget the thriller, which was going nowhere, and write the comedy instead. The student did so and wrote a passable comedy, though nothing special. He then felt able to concentrate on the thriller, which turned out to be excellent – far better than the comedy – so much so that it was taken up by a production company and became a success at the box office. Obviously he had needed to get the comedy out of his system before he was able to focus properly on the thriller. It was the thriller he was meant to write, and that became the success, but the long-term desire to write a comedy was getting in the way and he could not achieve the right state of mind.

I had the good fortune not only to learn from, but also to work with, a master of yoga, Dr George King. He was running The Aetherius Society a successful international organisation with thousands of members in groups all over the world, and as well as giving spiritual teaching and leadership to them, which he did brilliantly, he had to organise them. In a voluntary organisation, in which you are not hiring and firing people but trying to bring them together for a worthwhile purpose, this can be very complex indeed. It is made even more complex by the cultural and social differences between people in various parts of the world. Frequently, when a serious problem arose, he would appear to ignore it and concentrate on something much simpler and less important. Having dealt with that, he would come back to the important problem and deal with it quickly and effectively; he used the first problem as a way of focusing his mind before dealing with the main one.

Many lessons in mental attitudes can be drawn from sport. In golf for example, when you are teeing off, it makes no difference to your shot whether there is water in front of you or a clear and open fairway. Your shot should be exactly the same in either case and should go way beyond the water anyway. Psychologically, though, it can make all the difference in the world. The presence of water means that if you do a poor tee off, your ball will go into the water and you will have to tee off again losing two shots. If you do a poor shot, and the ball lands on the fairway, where there is no water, you carry on from the point where you land and lose no points. But this is only if you do a poor shot. You should not be intending to do a poor shot, and it should make no difference, physically at least, to how you play. It is all in the mind.

How many top sportsmen have got to the final match, in which the physical conditions are the same, and yet because of the importance of the match they lose their nerve and play badly. If it is a directly competitive sport such as tennis, there are obvious reasons for this – the balls are far more difficult to return when you are up against the best players, rallies go on for longer and so on. But it is also how you cope with the psychological pressure of winning. In a game such as snooker where you are playing alone in turns, it should make no difference at all. It is purely psychological at this stage. Chess, which is supposed to be a result of logical analysis, involves massive reserves of nervous and emotional energy at championship level. Problem-solving is achieved by first re-focusing and altering your mind set, then addressing the issue at hand.

WHAT WOULD THEY DO?

One way of re-focusing and altering your mind set, when there appears to be no solution to a problem, is to imagine how a wise person would deal with it. Of course we all have different ideas of who is wise, but there is general agreement that Jesus Christ, the Lord Buddha, Sri Krishna, Confucius and Gandhi would appear on any list of the wisest people to have walked the earth. I am sure you can think of others. The following meditation is very useful when you face a dilemma.

WISING UP

- *When facing a problem which appears to have no answer, or to which there are numerous possible solutions and you cannot decide which is correct, turn to a wise person for guidance.*

- *Select someone from history with whom you are familiar. You should know about their philosophy, life and approach to different situations.*

- *Imagine you are in their presence and are able to seek their advice. Pose the question and imagine their voice speaking to you, or a form of words written by them in front of you, whichever you prefer.*

- *Now imagine you are receiving an answer from them. Do not try to influence this answer with your own thoughts, but allow it to pop into your brain.*

- *Remember this is only your imagination – you are not actually making contact with them. What you are receiving is your impression of what they would say to you about the dilemma you are facing, based on your knowledge and understanding of their life.*

- *The more love and appreciation you feel for the wise person you have chosen, the better this exercise will work for you.*

SLEEP ON IT

An excellent way of relaxing the mind, and altering your mind set into one which is receptive to that part of you which knows the answer to the problem you are trying to solve, is sleep. It is not just an old wives' tale to 'sleep on it', it really works. It is important to remember that a part of you *does* know the answer to every problem – it is just a question of connecting with it. The answer can come in a flash of illumination, which only later is followed by a rational understanding of why this is the right answer. The following exercise can be a very effective way of clearing your mind and getting a better perspective on things. Although it is not strictly a meditation, it is best done in a meditative frame of mind. If you induce a meditative state of mind before going to bed, and then do this practice, it will be far more effective.

WAKING UP

- *Before going to bed at night, pose the unsolved question to yourself. There may just be a missing link which eludes you completely at the time.*

- *Having posed the question, try to detach from it. Do not ponder the whys and wherefores, but let your internal mechanism work to produce a solution.*

- *When you wake up, you may find you know the answer. If you do not, immediately pose it again and see what comes straight to you.*

- *An additional help can be to write the question down, as well as posing it mentally, and leave it by the side of your bed. When you wake up, immediately read it to yourself and see if the answer comes to you.*

As well as literally sleeping on it, you can metaphorically sleep on it by pausing in your deliberations. Instead of going over and over the problem in your mind in the tape loop syndrome, break the pattern of thought by doing something completely different. It might be a simple thing like getting up and doing the washing up. Then come back to it afresh. It is as though you are coaxing the answer out of the inner recesses of your mind. All the time you must be absolutely confident that there is an answer and you do know it. It is a cliché, but no less true for it, that problems were made to be overcome.

NEW PERSPECTIVES

It is incredible how things can seem so different in a different setting. When you are with certain people a situation can seem absolutely awful. In the cold light of day, when you are alone, it does not seem so bad at all; it was the negativity of those people which made the whole thing seem worse. One excellent way to alter your mind set is to alter your physical environment. It may not be possible to always drive to different locations in order to solve every problem, but you can do this mentally. You can imagine you are in your favourite location, sitting on a beach, walking in the country, or wherever it might be. Then, when you have built up in your imagination not only the visual scene, but also the sounds and smells of the place, pose the question to yourself again – it might suddenly seem much easier to deal with.

Here is a meditation you can use to find the answer to any question, not just to personal problems, but to spiritual and metaphysical issues which you may need guidance on.

OPEN DOOR

- *Imagine you are standing in front of a large door, a door that you would love to have in front of your own home.*

- *On the other side of the door is the answer you are seeking.*

- *Knock hard upon it, and as you do so frame the question to which you require an answer.*

- *Stop knocking and visualise the door slowly opening.*

- *As it does so a shaft of light pours through the opening which gets larger as the door opens further, bit by bit.*

- *When it is fully open you see pure light streaming through.*

- *Close your eyes and allow an answer to form in your mind, calmly waiting as it does so.*

- *When you have the answer, the door closes slowly and soundlessly in front of you.*

KEY 7

The Wealth Factor

USING MIND POWER TO make money is an extremely questionable business. It is done all the time, of course, very often by questionable businesses, and while it may work on a mental level, it will fail miserably on a karmic level. Using the power of your mind to convince somebody else to invest in what you want them to invest in, regardless of whether it is what they need or truly want, is a form of hypnotism which can rebound badly on you. You are liable to find yourself in a situation later when you invest in something you do not want or really need. Perhaps that is why they say that the easiest person to sell to is a salesman. Having said that, money is not, of itself, bad or the root of all evil. It is purely a form of energy. Greed is one of the roots of so-called evil; money is only a tool. It can be used selfishly for personal gain, or it can be used to do fantastic good for others. It is all down to motive.

➤ WALK THE WALK

Paradoxically, one of the best ways to make money is to spend it. That is the essence of Jesus' parable of the talents. Out of three servants who were given money by their master, two put it to work and made more, the other kept it and made nothing – in modern jargon he would have made a 'real terms loss' after allowing for inflation! Of course Jesus was talking about more than just making money – it was a parable of talents in general being used to their fullest extent. Opportunities need to be taken and abilities used before they amount to anything. There is a great American saying which differentiates between those who 'talk the talk' and those who 'walk the walk'. Theorists who just talk about things, discuss their ideas but never realise them, are not wealthy people. True wealth can only be measured in experience, i.e. those who walk the walk.

Being wealthy is patently not the same as having a lot of money; it is to do with how you feel. A multi-millionaire who has a desperate desire to be a billionaire does not feel rich. He is constantly comparing himself to billionaires and his lifestyle pales in his own eyes in comparison. In the same way that you are as young as you feel, you are also as rich as you feel. In ancient India, a fulfilled yogi, living in a cave with access to food, drink and clothing, was one of the wealthiest people on earth. To a materially-minded person the yogi's life would be considered bland, dull and impoverished. Yet the inner life of the yogi was filled with knowledge, ecstasy and purpose. He was rich in experience and untroubled by material concerns. That is wealth. Nowadays, when the spirit of the age has moved beyond personal development to focus on service to others as a priority, a wealthy person might be one who is fulfilled through caring for and actively helping others.

Selfishness cannot ever be satiated; service sets you free. Wealth, strangely enough, is the exact opposite of possession.

Of course, the millions of people who do not have what they need, who are living in poverty, are not free. They need help, and those who can afford to should give it to them. It is not shortage of cash which causes poverty, but the greed of those who keep more than they need.

⟩ POSSESSION IS NOT RECOGNISED UNDER KARMIC LAW

Lazy, untalented or spendthrift people who decry those who have worked hard with skill and diligence to become rich, have no credibility whatsoever. They are missing the point. Many people who become rich (though certainly not all) do so by their own efforts. They have, one way or another, earned their money. It does not mean, however, that they strictly own it. It is a form of energy. The possession of it is illusory; it exists as long as the mind set of the human race accepts that it exists. During his lifetime a Van Gogh painting was worth the price of a simple meal. The same painting nowadays would sell for millions of pounds. The painting has not changed, only the perception of it. Any financial valu-ation of that painting was and is completely unreal. A million pounds sterling would be completely worthless if all the other nations of the world decided not to recognise sterling any more. History is littered with market crashes in which commodities and currencies have lost their value overnight. It is going on in certain parts of the world even now. The price of this book might double tomorrow in some countries (I told you it was a good investment).

The Hindus have a great Sanskrit term for illusory things: 'maya'. In order to help their more advanced sannyasins (students) to find enlightenment they encourage them to see the material world as being composed of maya. This philos-ophy enables them to focus on the spiritual realities of existence without getting caught up in the many distractions of worldly life. They cultivate the quality of vairagya (detachment) which enables them to give their total focus to higher thought and practice. In the West, the monastery tradition, which incidentally has very little connection with the life and teaching of Jesus, was designed to take monks and nuns out of the everyday world so that they would not be affected by its worldliness. There has been a tradition of separateness among certain devotees of all the major religions. I believe that this is no longer necessary or desirable. The new millennium is a time for integration, coming together, and working in the world. It is now better to change things than to try to avoid them.

It is not money that is wrong, it is the misuse or underuse of it. It could, with spiritual direction, change the world completely for the better. Of course there would be extremely powerful, global, financial interests – far and away more powerful than any politicians in the world – who would violently (and I mean that literally) object. But, from a karmic point of view, the spiritual will always triumph in the end, despite all appearances.

⇘ RULES OF GIVE AND TAKE

To co-operate with karmic principles on wealth, I recommend the following rules of give and take.

- Whatever you regard as wealth – knowledge, power, relationships, money, consciousness, experience – you must be willing to share with others.

- As a Chinese proverb says: *if you love something, throw it to the wind; if it is blown back it is yours forever.* This means that you must be prepared to let go of your possessions and then, paradoxically enough, they will truly be yours. The Old Testament story of Abraham being asked by God to sacrifice his son Isaac has exactly the same meaning. Abraham's son and heir was his most cherished possession. As soon as he demonstrated that he was willing to let go of him, a ram appeared from the thicket and the sacrifice was no longer necessary.

- Karma is a law of necessity. What you need you get, and you are responsible for getting what you need. Some metaphysical teachings neglect the all-important element of practicality, which means taking care of material things as well as spiritual ones. It is one of the essential lessons of life in this physical world.

- Yogis like Vivekananda taught that you should never accept gifts. By this he meant that you should never receive without giving, either money or some other form of repayment. You might not be asked to do so, but the karmic law requires it one way or another.

- If you have a debt to someone, whether financial, emotional or any other, you will have to repay it somehow. If you try to avoid it, it will be extracted from you through experience.

- You need to value money because of what it can do, but never be ruled by it. Being rich adds a burden of responsibility, because you are then in a position to help save lives and prevent others from suffering. If you do not do so, but instead spend it on yourself and your family who are already comfortably off, you are responsible for that decision. The poor person is not so responsible, because they could not have helped in this way.

THE ALCHEMY OF WEALTH

Alchemists from the Middle Ages onwards were perceived as people in pursuit of wealth. The theory went that they had discovered a means of turning base metal into gold. It may be that many alchemists allowed this belief to persist, because it was safer for them than the real truth coming out. Mystics in the West had to keep their practices shrouded in mystery for fear of their lives at the hands of the Inquisition or some other bigoted court. In fact, they were in pursuit of another elixir known variously as the fifth element, the philosopher's stone, the holy grail, and many other names. They were certainly involved in transmutation, but base metal into gold was only a symbol; they wished to transmute physical forces in general into spiritual ones.

Certainly there were charlatans around posing as alchemists, who conned people out of money on vague promises of greater wealth. This is well illustrated in Ben Jonson's play, *The Alchemist*, written in 1610. The same is true today, and not just among some who claim to be psychics and mystics – look no further than the city of London, where conmen mingle freely with legitimate traders. But there were many genuine mystics in Western Europe, such as Jonson's great contemporary, Sir Francis Bacon, who cloaked his real work behind a rather unsuccessful political career. Many of them looked back to the mysterious, ancient Egyptian god, Thoth, who became known as Hermes Trismegistus, the self-same figure as the god Mercury in ancient Rome. The philosophy of Hermes was one of transmutation – not to detach from worldliness as the yogis taught in their philosophy of maya, but to transmute it. The yogis were intent on getting as far away from the basic physical world as possible and would spend as much of their life as possible on higher planes of thought and existence. Hermes, who reputedly lived many thousands of years ago and is regarded, among other things, as the person who introduced writing to ancient Egypt (through hieroglyphics), is a symbol of a different type of approach, and one which I believe is far more relevant, in many ways, to the new millennium: *instead of trying to rise above this physical world, try to change it.*

AN INVOCATION

- **Physical** *Analyse your needs as opposed to your desires. Identify something you genuinely need in order to fulfil your life's destiny.*

- **Mental** *Having identified it – and this will only work if it is something you genuinely need to complete your purpose in life – visualise it coming to you.*

- **Spiritual** *Be thankful to the universal provider for receiving it. If you have no religious beliefs, just be thankful to the universe generally from which all life and energy comes.*

- *At no point must you visualise any other specific person being affected by this practice, or you will be attempting to control them, which could backfire on you.*

- *Have full confidence that what you have visualised will happen through the three steps of (1) careful analysis, which brings discrimination; (2) visualisation, which places a demand; and (3) thankfulness for receiving it, which brings balance.*

- *Then completely let go of the thing you have invoked. There is no saying when it will come to you. If it does not do so, it may be that you did not need it in the first place.*

It is a platitude, but still true, that you cannot take your money with you when you go. My experience of contact with people who have died indicates that they are no longer very concerned with how rich they were when they were physically alive, but far more with what they did for others. Even giving money does not always help the people you give it to, as can be seen from some of the super-rich who inherit fortunes and end up in misery. More than money, wealth is knowledge, power, influence, energy, health, friendship, love and the opportunity to serve. Some of those things you can take with you when you die. At the same time, you could have all those things and still not be fulfilled. A successful life is not about what you have got, it is about what you do with it.

THE SECOND EYE

Keys of Intuition

KEY 8

Picking Up Thoughts

HOW MANY TIMES HAVE you thought something, and immediately somebody nearby has said exactly the same? Not vaguely the same type of thing, but the exact same words. How many times have you thought of someone and just as you did so the telephone rang and it was them? If you had been expecting them to call, it could be discounted as a coincidence, but you were not. In fact you had not seen them for five years at least and had hardly thought of them at all until now. Or you thought of someone who has no particular significance to you, walked out of the house and bumped into them in the street.

These types of incidents are going on all the time and cynics who dismiss them as coincidental are flying in the face of evidence. The Koestler Institute at Edinburgh University, which is examining the evidence for parapsychology, ran a trial involving more than 100 people. They found that subjects were often able to pick out which of four pictures were being telepathically 'beamed' to them by someone in the next room. The images were picked randomly by a computer and subjects had a success rate of almost 50 per cent – twice the 25 per cent rate expected if they were guessing. The chances of doing this by fluke alone are around a staggering 1 in 14 million. Typically, scientists regard a fluke whose odds are less than 1 in 20 as being 'significant'. By those standards, the findings by the Koestler Institute, which were revealed to a meeting of the British Psychological Society in April 1997, were almost one million times more convincing than some conventional scientific evidence. Other institutions such as the Psychophysical Research Laboratories in Princeton, New Jersey, USA, the Institute for Parapsychology in North Carolina, USA, and the University of Amsterdam have also produced compelling evidence for telepathy in experiments which showed that the incidence of accuracy was consistently above chance.

One of the most sensational pieces of evidence emerged from de-classified CIA papers, which showed that the US Government has been conducting secret research programmes in ESP (extra-sensory perception). Papers revealed by the Society for Scientific Exploration in California show that startlingly accurate results have been obtained. The program's founder and first director, laser physicist Hal Puthoff, stated: 'The integrated results appear to provide unequivocal evidence of a human capacity to access events remote in space and time, however falteringly, by some cognitive process not yet understood.' Another leading scientist involved in the programme, Russell Targ, gave details of an experiment performed in 1973 in which a psychic was able to pinpoint the exact location of a secret Soviet research and development laboratory. This feat was later verified by satellite photography. Professor Jessica Utts, a statistician at the University of California who examined the CIA files, was so convinced by the evidence that she stated: 'I believe that it would be wasteful of valuable resources to continue to look for proof ... Resources should be directed to the pertinent questions about how this ability works.'

The most pertinent of these questions is how to induce the state of mind which will open you up to the latent psychic abilities within all of us. So-called primitive races are often far more attuned to their natural ESP, firstly because they use it more and secondly because they lead a less left-hand-brain dominated life; they do not rely on phones, faxes, computers and so on, which require an analytical faculty to operate them. Time pressures can also be more fluid – in short, people 'flow' more with life. This allows them not only to receive impressions, but to take notice of them. In the hustle and bustle of modern technological life, very little attention is paid to the intuitive impulses which exist, if only we would listen to them. Meditation takes us into another state of consciousness in which we are more receptive to ESP, providing it is taken beyond the stage of simple relaxational therapy. It can be the key to far more than this.

➢ SUBJECTIVELY SPEAKING

There is no substitute for personal experience. You can argue objectively until you are blue in the face, but you will never convince someone who does not wish to be convinced. You can demonstrate the ability to bend spoons, for example, but do very little good for anybody – they either believe you or they do not. If they do not wish to believe you, they will regard you as a showman, no different from David Copperfield or Paul Daniels, and you have proved nothing to them. If they do believe you, they will still learn nothing whatsoever about themselves. They will just regard you as being psychic, but have no particular reason to think that they could also demonstrate these abilities. Anyway, there are far better uses for psychic powers than damaging cutlery!

Intuition is a marvellous faculty and should be treated with at least the same respect as the classical philosophers treated the faculty of reason. It is regarded by some as a divine gift. It also has the association of being a particularly feminine quality, which contains a degree of truth. Women are generally more expert at the art of feeling, though some men can be highly intuitive too. Intuition is all about feeling rather than thinking. The Keys of Imagination utilise the conscious mind, and the all-important power of visualisation. The Keys of Intuition go beyond this and start to awaken the superconscious mind, using the deeper contemplative abilities.

RECEPTION MODE

- *Adopt the usual posture and practise some deep and even breathing for a couple of minutes.*

- *On the in-breath, visualise white light entering the whole of your body and on the out-breath, feel cleansed.*

- *Start to watch your mind as though your brain was a radio receiver. Do not think about anything in particular, but become aware of the thoughts and feelings flowing in and out of your brain. Do not attach to any of them, and certainly do not try to rationalise them; just let go of them.*

- *Now focus your mind on the room you are sitting in. See if any thoughts start to come to you about the room. Go beyond the room and into the whole building, not trying to pry into any specific matter, but just receiving whatever comes to you.*

- *If you find this difficult, put out a mental request to receive the thoughts and feelings within the building and see what comes to you.*

- *If you pick up specific feelings, images, names or any other details, make a mental note of them, and after the exercise write them down. You may find them to be accurate impressions of events, people or moods connected with the past history of your room or the building as a whole.*

⤳ TRIAL AND ERROR

The only way to learn how to pick up thoughts accurately is by doing it; sooner or later you have to take this leap. It is not a leap of faith because you should remain questioning (though never cynical) in the early stages of your progression. As you develop, you will gain greater confidence and will be able to discriminate between what is accurate and what is not. Ideally, you need one or more friends to practise with, who are equally keen to learn.

TWO-WAY CONNECTION

- *Be seated with another person for this exercise. Place your right palms together to bring about a connection between the two of you.*

- *One of you is the receiver and the other the transmitter.*

- *The receiver starts to watch the thoughts and feelings flowing in and out of their own mind.*

- *The transmitter draws in white light on the in-breath and on the out-breath sends it down his or her arms, through the palm and into the receiver for a few minutes. This creates a more solid link between the two.*

- *The transmitter stops doing this and starts to send a very general, universal thought. It can be anything, but it should not be too specific. For example, it should be plants in general, rather than a sycamore tree. When you start it should be as easy as possible. If you become skilled you can make it more specific and difficult.*

- *The receiver watches their own mind and notes an image which recurs or is very strong.*

- *After several minutes of this, the receiver tells the transmitter*

what images, if any, he or she has picked up. If any of them
are accurate or closely related to what has been transmitted,
try to remember how you felt when you picked these up. If
they are not accurate, try to remember those feelings too. This
way you will start to learn how it feels when you are accu-
rate.

You can practise tuning into thoughts wherever you go and
with whomever you meet. For example, when you receive a
letter in the post, instead of opening it immediately, pause for
a moment. Hold the envelope in your hands, between your
fingers, before opening it. Become a receiver for the thoughts
which are impressed in the letter inside the envelope, and see
if you can identify its general mood. You may know who it is
from, in which case see whether anything comes to you
which you could not have known intellectually. It may be in
picture form, in which case make a mental note of whatever
you see in your mind's eye, or it may be a form of words, in
which case see if anything close to this is contained in the
letter. If you do not know who it is from, see if you can pick
up what sort of person it might be, and if possible the exact
identity. Do not do this as a guessing game, but as a real
impression of what the letter might be about. If you are right,
try to remember the process as it came to you. Note how you
felt when you got an accurate impression. If it was wrong,
likewise note the feelings and impressions you received,
which turned out to be imaginary. With practice you will
start to tell the difference between genuine intuition and pure
imagination.

When the phone or the doorbell ring, try to do the same.
See if something flashes into your mind at that moment
which has any connection with the person who turns out to
be there. Before watching the news on television, see if any
unexpected nations or situations come into your mind, which
turn out to have a connection with the news. If they do, and
it would have been an unlikely guess, again note your feel-

ings. All the time you are trying to get into the groove of intuition. By trial and error you will start to identify what it feels like to be in this groove, and eventually you will be able to pick up thoughts whenever you choose to.

↘ SWITCHING OFF

People with a natural intuitive gift frequently ask me how they can learn to switch off. You do not always want to be open to every impression in the atmosphere. For example, if you are visiting a sick friend or relative in hospital, the last thing you want to do is receive the vibrations from all the patients there who are experiencing feelings of pain. By the time you reached the patient you were visiting, you would be in no state to be of any help or comfort to them – you would be too de-tuned by the vibrations you had picked up along the way. If you find this happening and you start to feel drained and affected by outside vibrations when you do not wish to, perform the Battery Charger Exercise (see page 51).

You can determine when you want to be receptive and when you do not. You can switch the mind into one of two different modes: the active or the receptive. The ancient manual used by adepts in China, known as the *I Ching*, draws clearly on this distinction. Composed of 64 sections called hexagrams, this superb work utilises the yin (receptive) and the yang (creative) in every possible permutation of six – from six of just one, all the way through every numerical breakdown, to six of the other. As well as being an excellent way of developing your intuition and bringing guidance into your life, the *I Ching* contains a wealth of philosophical teaching about life. It also shows how the mind functions, from fully creative, through all the combinations to completely receptive. With practice, you will get used to switching from one to the other as and when you choose. There is, after all, one force within the human psyche which is even greater than mind power – your will. It is of course linked to the mind, but goes beyond it. Using the power of concentration you can determine the focus for your intuition and will gradually be able to switch it on and off.

KEY 9

Understanding People

YOU CAN KNOW SOMEONE for years and still be surprised by their behaviour, yet others whom you have only just met you can read like a book; you know just how they are going to react to any given situation. Some people have an instant rapport with you; others, no matter how long or hard you try, you just cannot get through to. There are several possible reasons for this. It could be a result of past life associations – you have known a person in a previous life, and although the situation may be very different now, you have not lost this unconscious knowledge of what makes them tick. It could be that you have a lot of mutual interests, or that you have a similar background, education and upbringing. Or it could be that you just agree with them on many points and that makes it easier to read where they are coming from and how they are likely to react. Some people put it all down to 'chemistry'.

◆ CHEMISTRY BETWEEN PEOPLE

Chemistry is a science based on relationships, in which chemical combinations bring reactions of different kinds. Combinations of people have exactly the same effect, either on a personal or working basis. There are numerous groups and double acts in the world of entertainment which have worked brilliantly, yet on their own the individuals were not nearly as effective. Something happens when they come together which is more than the sum of several talents; another factor emerges from the chemical reaction between them. The same is true of personal relationships. If you are with a couple who are in love, who blend well together and are happy, the effect is magnetic on all those around them (unless they are the type of couple who live in their own world and are oblivious of everybody else). If, on the other hand you are with a couple who are not in love, who are together from expediency, fear of being alone or some pragmatic motive only, you can feel a certain lifelessness. Alone they can be happy, motivated people, together they create a negativity from the chemical reaction between them. This is very noticeable in the case of a marriage which has broken down, and yet the partners have not faced up to the situation, and are carrying on together out of habit.

It takes more than just chemistry to keep a relationship of any kind going. Just as important is understanding, and this can be very difficult at times. When communication has broken down between two people, ridiculous things are often said – things which neither person really means. By stepping back at that point and tuning in to the other person, instead of mentally going through a tape loop of repeated memories and problems connected with them, the situation can be resolved. The chemical reactions can be transmuted into a more loving energy. You will be able to see eye to eye with them again – the metaphysical meaning of that phrase being the attunement of the individuals' inner or psychic eyes. It does not necessarily mean agreeing on all points, it is about a general rapport with each other. The same principle underlying all meditation techniques of tuning your mind like a receiver set applies to relationships between people. If one person is on 'long wave' and the other on 'short wave', no communication is possible between the two. Both have to adjust their own receiver sets and agree to meet on 'medium wave' to create a degree of understanding between them. Very often this is done by getting a third party, for example a counsellor, to act as a go-between or even a catalyst. It can also be done by both people meditating on the causes of the breakdown and then deciding together on a course of action, which might be an amicable parting of the ways or a resolution to work constructively together in future. Even if there is still disagreement, this very process should bring greater understanding between them. Here is a four-part technique followed by a meditation for fixing relationships, which has to be done wholeheartedly by both parties to work effectively.

FIXING RELATIONSHIPS

(1) Analysis

- *Think back to your original meeting with the other person. Was there an immediate rapport between you – a chemistry – or did you have to work on it to make it gradually emerge?*

- *If you are married or committed to the other person, were you absolutely sure in your heart when you made the commitment that you were doing the right thing, with no nagging doubt in the back of your mind?*

- *Have you ever been completely sure that you loved them?*

- *If the answer to all three questions is 'no', you have some difficult problems to surmount. It may be that you are trying to unnaturally create a relationship with someone for* intellectual reasons, when in fact there is no basis for it to work.

- If the answer to any of the questions is 'yes', you have some foundation on which to re-build the relationship if you both want to.

(2) Detachment

- Observe your own mental patterns. See if they go round and round in your brain like a tape loop.

- You will find that many of the thoughts, possibly tinged with bitterness, regret and other emotions, are irrelevant to the future. Let them go.

- See which thoughts come back and stay with you. They will be the unresolved incidents which are still relevant to the future.

- Look at those thoughts from the other person's point of view as impartially as you can. They may then fade from relevance.

- See what, if any, issues are left.

(3) Coming Together

- Calmly tell each other the issues which remain, if any – see if they are the same ones.

- If you cannot immediately resolve these issues, agree to drop them.

- If you both want to stay together, and you have resolved or agreed to drop the issues between you, visualise in silence your future relationship being harmonious.

- Surround yourselves mentally in a green light, a colour of harmony and balance.

- Think back to a happy occasion when you were in harmony and recapture the feeling of that time.

- *Feel a positive atmosphere build up as you allow these thoughts to transmute the destructive energies which have gone between you.*

(4) Meditation

- *Sit together with your right palms in contact with each other.*

- *Allow an interchange of vibrations through the palms of the hands while you breathe deeply and evenly.*

- *Now let all the previous parts of the exercise go, as if your thoughts were being dissolved in a mist of white light which surrounds you both.*

- *Observe your thoughts and see what comes into your mind. You will probably gain a better insight into each other's feelings.*

- *Together you will start to build up a new pattern of energies and the problems of the past will disappear as you establish a focus of oneness. Just the fact that you are meditating will enable this to start happening.*

➤ LOVE POWER

Love is more than an emotion; it is an energy which can be transmitted from one person to another. It is a healing force, and often one which is very much misunderstood. All living beings react to this energy, whether they are consciously aware of it or not. Experiments have been done on plants which show that when they are sent love in the form of a blessing or prayer, they prosper. In 1967, Dr Robert N. Miller, professor of chemical engineering at Georgia Institute of Technology in Atlanta, conducted a series of long-distance prayer-plant tests. He used ordinary rye grass and a rotary electromechanical transducer connected to a strip chart recorder, a device which had been used at the US

Department of Agriculture for measuring plant growth. The tip of a leaf of a plant was attached to the counter-balanced lever arm, which in turn was connected to the transducer. As the plant grew the lever arm moved and generated an electrical signal which caused a deflection on the chart recorder. The normal growth rate of a new blade of rye grass was established as being 6.25 thousands of an inch per hour. When prayer was sent to the rye grass from 600 miles away by healers who visualised it being surrounded by white light, the rate increased to 52.5 thousands of an inch per hour – an increase of 840 per cent. The same principle is even true of inanimate objects. People who love their cars as more than just an inanimate object with a functional purpose, often find that they respond to this energy, that they perform better for it. Naturally, this is hard to prove, but there are those who will swear blind that it is true.

It all depends what you mean by 'love'. Some people mean 'I need you', 'I want to possess you' or 'I desire your body', when they say 'I love you'. Most pop songs, for instance, stay around that level. This is not the highest or the truest meaning of the word, which actually involves giving to others, and wanting to help others. They may be your partner, a relative or someone you have never met. Being gregarious and having lots of friends is not necessarily a sign that you are a loving person. You could be almost a recluse and still be filled with an overwhelming love for humanity. It is amazing, for example, just how many of the world's most famous philosophers lived without a partner, including, as far as we know, the following: Anselm, Aquinas, Bacon, Eckhart, Ockham, Erasmus, Hobbes, Descartes, Pascal, Malebranche, Newton, Leibniz, Locke, Hume, Kant, Schopenhauer, Kierkegaard, Nietzsche, Spinoza and Wittgenstein. Yet they all dedicated their lives to creating works for the betterment of humanity. This is not only true of philosophers; among the great composers, Beethoven, who never married despite rumours of his affairs, spoke of his overwhelming love for humanity, while Brahms went so far as to state that family life would detract from his vocation to write music. Others, such as Wagner, spoke of the inspiration he gained from, in his case, his second marriage.

Love is not the product of any particular personality. Someone, with charming manners and gushing affectations, might be almost devoid of it, while a brusque, tactless loner might be the very person to turn to when you really need help. Nor is it related to sexuality; pleasure-seeking Lotharios (of both sexes) generally leave more pain than love behind them. Most of the philosophers listed above were not only single, but also probably celibate. Nowadays, many people would assume that they must have been gay, because chastity has little currency in the modern world. Victorian bigotry is being replaced with a new type of prejudice: that all fulfilled people require a partner and children. It does not matter so much whether they make a success of it, as long as they have done it. Bachelors and spinsters tend to be regarded with suspicion by this new form of narrow-mindedness. But neither the Victorian prejudices nor the modern ones have anything to do with true love, which extends beyond the confines of any type of relationship, to a global and even cosmic level. Nothing visible is more deserving of our love than the sun, because without it we definitely could not exist. And if that sounds like a far-out concept, I must point out that it is one of the most ancient and widely held beliefs in the history of earth.

Love can be radiated without hugs, kisses or even so much as an introduction; you can do it all the time. You can become a silent radiator of this energy while sitting on a train or walking down the road, and people will be affected by it without even realising. As Lao-Tzu said, the greatest person is the one who has such an effect that people change, but think they did it themselves.

LOVE: THE TRANSMUTER

- *Breathe deeply and evenly for a few moments.*

- *Visualise someone whom you associate with love. Jesus or Buddha would be two excellent choices, or you may have a particular person who represents love to you.*

- *Imagine the individual you have chosen as though you were sitting in their presence. Draw in and absorb the vibrations around them, until you are imbued with their loving presence.*

- *Now think about people whom you know, particularly any you have had a disagreement or misunderstanding with, and maintain the feeling of love you have drawn into yourself.*

- *This should change the situation between you and them for the better. The next time you see them, try to maintain this feeling of love in their presence.*

➤ EQUALITY

The injustices of history have turned equality into the ultimate value of modern times. Indeed, the United States is founded on the notion that all men are created equal. Democracy is rightly cherished, but wrongly regarded as a passport to correct decision-making; the popularity of Nazism alone proved that the people's choice is not necessarily correct. There is a difference between having the right and being right. People are patently not equal, and it is arguable that all people do not have the same degree of right to vote. Is the opinion of someone who has devoted his or her life to charitable works equally as valid as that of a repeated child molester? Should they both have the same say in the affairs of a nation?

There is a part of every person which is exactly equal with every other person on earth, however: that is their potential. We all have the potential of perfection. Whatever we have or have not done, we can all change and rise up fully to the occasion. Saint Paul persecuted Christians and then became one of the greatest saints. Whatever your views of Saint Paul and Christianity, this shows the fantastic potential within all of us to achieve whatever goals we determine, whatever we may have been or done in the past. This type of outlook brings tolerance. Not so much tolerance that we actually condone wrong behaviour, but enough to see the fantastic potential within all people, to avoid becoming arrogant or self-centred, and to gain a real understanding of all people, regardless of their age, sex, race or religion – even if it is not exactly the same as our own!

KEY 10

Interpreting Your Dreams

S RI PATANJALI, THE FATHER of Raja Yoga (the yoga of psychic and mental control), said in his aphorisms, composed well over 2,000 years ago, that extraordinary perceptions can be obtained by fixing your mind upon a dream experience. Some people talk incessantly about their dreams, without trying to understand what they really mean, and all too often they get it wrong; one person's ladder of evolution is another person's fear of climbing too high, and so on. Books on the subject abound, but even they do not always hold consistent information. I believe meditation is the answer to this highly contentious subject. The measurement of brain wave patterns, which I referred to in 'A Workout for the Mind', indicates a link between the meditative state and the dream state. In both, the frequency of brain wave emission has slowed from the normal active beta state to a slower state. Through meditating and consciously inducing this slower pattern of brain waves, and thereby deeper levels of perception, you will be able to tap into the inner meanings of your dreams.

✤ DREAMS AND THE UNCONSCIOUS

Psychoanalysts will argue that they have an exclusive insight into the world of the unconscious, but even they do not agree with each other. Emphasis on sexual repression, parental influence, experiences in the womb and, occasionally, past life regression, varies from practitioner to practitioner. Their biggest limitation, in my view, is focusing solely on the subconscious function of the mind and ignoring the super-conscious. According to an ICM poll conducted for the *Daily Mail* in 1998, 19 per cent of British adults have had dreams which predicted the future. These figures are broken down as 17 per cent of men and 21 per cent of women. This stagger-ing result by a top polling organisation shows that literally millions of people in Britain claim to have experienced what is undoubtedly a psychic phenomenon. Even if, in the inter-ests of compromise, you eliminate some of them as being coincidental (not that I personally believe in coincidence), and others as being liable to have happened anyway, the figures are too high to ignore the obvious fact that many people see the future in their dreams.

This is no surprise to me, because I have received numer-ous letters and phone calls over the years from people from all walks of life, attesting to such experiences. They have absolutely no reason to make them up. Some of them are mundane, some beautiful, others tragic. One lady phoned me on a radio phone-in and described a dream in which she had seen her newly-born baby die in a few days time. This had not been predicted medically, and for her must have been the most horrific dream imaginable. Psychoanalysts might have put it down to a subconscious fear caused in her childhood. But a week later, completely unexpectedly, the baby contracted a serious illness and died. She asked me what the reason could be for a dream like that – after all, it did not alter the outcome. I asked her whether by going through the pain of the dream, it in some way prepared her for the event

THE SECOND EYE

when it actually happened, and made it just a bit easier to cope. She told me that it definitely did. Perhaps that was her answer.

Cases like this demonstrate that dreams are not just the result of the subconscious mind. When the conscious part of the brain is inactive during sleep, another part takes over. Often this is the subconscious expressing itself through imagery, but there are two other possibilities. The first is an out-of-body or astral experience, which I will explain fully in Key Eighteen. The other is an intuitive experience brought on by the superconscious mind. Because the conscious mind is inhibited by sleep, under certain conditions this highest and most spiritual aspect of your mind can flourish. This can either lead to a pre-cognitive dream, where a future event is revealed, or a visionary dream with a symbolic meaning about your destiny or life path. The difference between this and a subconscious dream is that it will reveal information which is not contained in your subconscious, such as the motivation of another person, a premonition about the future or some other intuitively derived knowledge. Often dreams will be a mixture of some or all of these phenomena, including subconscious impressions, as they ramble from one thing to another. On other occasions you may have a lucid dream, which is purely inspired by your subconscious. It varies from person to person, and each one needs to be interpreted individually, rather than from some theoretical blueprint.

➤ IMAGES IN DREAMS

Poets such as T.S. Eliot realised that apparently unrelated images, like the smell of tobacco and a sunset for example, could be used powerfully in poems to evoke instinctive reactions. These are brought about by the subconscious associations people have with these images. Surrealist painters started to use the same thing in their art. But there was one fatal flaw in this concept: the smell of tobacco and the sunset invoke one set of impressions in one person and another set in another person. Tobacco may subliminally remind one person of their beloved grandfather, and another of lung cancer, so the effect will be entirely different. In dream interpretation, this means that guides on the subject are about as useful as the astrological forecasts, based only on sun signs, which are published in the press. They are wild generalisations, which are almost inapplicable at an individual level. Dream interpretation should be done, as it was in biblical days for example by Joseph (wearer of the multi-coloured coat), on a one-on-one basis. As with any form of divination, it is useful to have an exchange of information between the diviner and the person being divined to be sure of a correct interpretation. You can then ascertain what it actually means to that person, rather than basing it on some manual of dream symbols which will give you a general idea only. With this health warning in mind, here are five images, based on the five elements of creation, and their general meanings in dreams. Please remember that these only apply to dreams which are not genuine astral experiences.

- **Water** This represents the emotional side of life. If it is calm in the dream, it denotes a peaceful time (unless it is in any way stagnant). If it is turbulent, it suggests upset and trauma. Being buffeted around in water indicates that you are not coping emotionally; floating calmly suggests that you are. Being parched, or a lack of water, suggests a need for more feeling in your life; drowning suggests you need to free yourself emotionally.

- **Fire** Fire represents inspirational, instinctive and passionate behaviour. A warm burning flame suggests that these things are present in your life; an extinguished flame indicates that you need more of them, that something in your life has died. If a fire is out of control it signals danger, perhaps passions have been aroused too much. If it is a positive presence in the dream, it could indicate that you have creative opportunities.

- **Air** This element is generally represented by the wind, though it can manifest itself as breathing. It represents the mental, deductive and intuitive processes. A cool breeze on a warm day suggests refreshing thoughts are coming your way, while a gale, heavy gust or draught suggests unhelpful and uncontrolled thinking. If you cannot catch your breath, you are in need of the right knowledge; if you are breathing peacefully and deeply you have found some profound wisdom.

- **Earth** This represents practicality, common sense and realism. If you are standing on firm foundations, you have a good, practical basis; if you are on shifting sands or even sinking in quicksand, you need to be practical and sort your affairs out. If you are being buried, you are too mundane and concerned with the material things of life; if you are floating and cannot, try as you might, come down to earth, you need to turn your attention to material affairs.

- **Supernatural** If you can do things in your dream which are not usually possible, such as flying, healing, telekinesis (moving objects with thoughts), seeing or hearing further than your eyes or ears would normally be able to, there is an indication of the fifth, etheric element. If these abilities are easy for you in dreams, perhaps you should develop mystical abilities in your waking state. It may indicate that you are embarking on a spiritual quest within yourself. If they are out of control, you need the right training before going any further.

⮞ MEDITATING ON DREAMS

The first thing you need to ascertain, before any interpretation of a dream is possible, is what type of dream you had.

Was it a completely cohesive experience in vivid techni-colour, during which you had what was tantamount to a real experience? If so, it was probably an astral experience, espe-cially if you returned directly to your physical body and woke up immediately, even in the middle of the night, rather than remembering it the next day. Was it a lucid dream, possibly in technicolour, which was essentially symbolic or about the future? If so, it was probably an intuitive or pre-cognitive dream. Was it a haphazard, nonsensical dream, which had some kind of inherent logic of its own? If you were eating your favourite food in prison with a particular friend of yours who could suddenly only speak an unintelligible foreign language, and then you found yourself drowning in a goldfish bowl (admittedly an exaggerated example), it would be a dream emanating from your subconscious. Finally, you might have had a dream which just rambled from one thing to another so much that it could not even be summarised as I have done here, and may therefore be virtually impossible to interpret constructively.

There is, of course, one thing you need to do before cat-egorising your dream into one of the above, and that is to remember it. The best way to do that is to reflect, as soon as you wake up or as early as you possibly can, upon the night's sleep. Leave your mind open and see what comes back to you. The following meditation exercise will enable you to remem-ber, categorise and interpret your dreams.

A DREAMSCAPE

- *As soon as possible after waking up, sit in a hard-backed chair and practise deep and even breathing.*

- *Make a mental request to recall any significant dream, and practise watchfulness. Allow images to appear on a screen in front of you.*

- *If nothing comes back to you after a while, it may be that there was nothing significant to remember, or that it is locked within your subconscious mind. Let it go and do a different meditation practice.*

- *If a dream does come back to you, review it in your mind. Decide which of the categories it falls into. Follow your intuition as well as your logic when deciding this.*

- *Having determined the category, review the elements of the dream. What do they mean to you, and what is their general significance? See whether any impressions come to you about the dream.*

- *If there are things you still cannot work out, just make a mental or written note and allow time to throw more light upon it. Very often dreams are triggers for other realisations, which will come to you gradually over time. By performing this practice, you have started the ball rolling, you have placed a demand upon your unconscious mind, and if you leave yourself open, answers will gradually filter through.*

- *If the dream is very emotive, you have to be able to detach from what you would like it to mean and concentrate only upon what it really does mean.*

- *The more you are willing to act upon your dream interpretation, the better it will work for you. If you have blockages, they will stand in the way of a clear meaning being revealed. You need self-honesty to interpret your own dreams.*

If you wish to follow a dream manual, it will still be beneficial to perform the above practice as well. Intuition will always throw light on any subject above and beyond intellectual information. You may only want to do this when a particular dream is troubling you. Just by attempting to interpret it, you will start your mind working down a certain line which, sooner or later, with diligent practice, will lead to meanings coming to you quicker and quicker until you no longer need to specifically meditate because it is immediately clear to you. Always keep a sense of humour about dreams; they are often quite boring to others. And never make them a substitute for being awake, because ultimately this is where the action is!

KEY 11

Tuning into Crystals

From sacred stones, standing stones and the philosopher's stone, to crystal therapy, crystal gazing and the magical power of quartz, there is a mystery in stones which can only truly be solved by using intuition. Only by tuning in can you fully experience the amazing effect which stones can have. The best way to appreciate the innate qualities of stones is to do so in a meditative state, so that you feel the different essences of each one.

➤ MYSTICAL PROPERTIES

All stones have mystical properties, particularly gems. They have the ability to store subtle energies, and, just as different colours have different healing effects, so different stones are more conducive to certain types of energy than others. The mystery of stones is not so much in their appearance or surface look, beautiful though that is, but in the energy contained within them. The vibrations radiated by stones are not always evident and can be unexpected. Take just three examples: the diamond, which, according to spectroscopic analysis, stores the colour indigo, represents the spiritual threshold through which the higher states are gained. It is the summation of all the practical qualities and attributes of the other colours, which results in a razor-sharp perception combined with practical idealism and clarity of mind. Just as it is used for sharpening tools, it is associated with the sharpening of the mind. Hence, Tibetan Buddhism's Vadjrayana path, which is the path of enlightenment through direct perception, is also known as the 'diamond' path.

The ruby is regarded as symbolic of the Ajna Chakra or 'third eye', representing enhanced vision. To this day, Hindu ladies paint a red dot in this position, the colour to which the ruby vibrates, even though many do not make this connection. Concentrating light through a ruby, thereby enhancing the distance and accuracy of the beam, created the first laser beams. The emerald is particularly misunderstood, being associated, like the colour green, with envy (just as blue is wrongly associated with depression). In fact, the emerald represents the exact opposite: harmony, balance, adaptability and positive discrimination. Of all stones, the most powerful from a magnetic point of view is one which has no specific colour associated with it, namely quartz crystal.

✒ HEALING WITH CRYSTALS

The main quality of quartz crystal is its ability to store vibrations. Early radios, known as crystal sets, used quartz to attract radio waves, which were then tuned to different frequencies by an electrical device. The same principle applies to spiritual vibrations, which can be transmitted through any system of energy healing. There is only one life force, though it goes under many different names. In crystal healing, this life force is conditioned by love, thought power and visualisation, but instead of being sent directly to the patient it is first stored in a crystal. This also applies to blessed stones in rings or other items. Dr King, for example, would bless stones from various holy mountains, which were then mounted on significant wooden shapes, such as crosses, triangles and circles. These have been used by hundreds of people for healing, inspiration and other spiritual qualities, which were specifically contained in the original blessings. He also pioneered the manufacture of crystal-based apparatus, which he called spiritual energy batteries, which have been used to store the energy invoked through prayer and mantra in a mission called Operation Prayer Power. Once stored, this energy is released at a later date to a specific trouble-spot in the world, such as an earthquake, hurricane or war zone, to bring mass healing.

As well as being used for energy storage and release, crystals can be used to enhance healing in the following way.

CRYSTAL HEALING

- *Select a suitable piece of quartz, which should be natural, i.e. it will have six sides with a terminated point. Sizes vary, but it should be at least three inches long and small enough to hold easily in one hand.*

- *Before using any piece of crystal, try to tune into its natural vibrations. Only if you find them to be positive should it be used for healing. If you pick up any negative feelings, do not use it for this purpose.*

- *Start by cleansing the crystal by placing it under a cold running tap for at least a minute. Make sure your hands are clean.*

- *Hold the quartz at the base with the point facing away from you. Start deep and even breathing, visualising yourself being filled with white light on the in-breath, and this light flowing down your arm, through the hand and into the crystal on the out-breath.*

- *Spiritual energy will start to flow naturally through the crystal towards the point and outwards, which will cleanse it further.*

- *Then, for a few minutes, hold the crystal near to, but not in physical contact with, the solar plexus of the person you want to heal. It would not be advisable to bring the crystal into physical contact with any specific ailment. If in doubt, send the healing over a distance.*

- *Cleanse the crystal again by placing it under a cold running tap and visualising white light flowing through it as you did before use. To be absolutely certain, you can further cleanse it by placing it under a light with a violet-coloured bulb or filter.*

➤ CRYSTAL MEDITATION

Crystals provide a constant supply of electro-magnetic energy which has an effect on the environment, especially at a psychic level. Everything in creation has a psychic counterpart, usually called the aura or etheric body. The natural energies, which flow throughout the cosmos, are easily channelled into and through crystals, thereby altering the mind set around them. This can be beneficial to meditation, providing the crystals are used correctly. I recommend the following procedure if you wish to use crystals to complement your meditation exercises.

CRYSTALLISING THE ATMOSPHERE

- *Select one or more crystals of any size, which you intuitively consider radiate positive energies. If possible, use larger crystals for this purpose, and use them for nothing else.*

- *Cleanse them as described in the previous exercise, and*

charge them with white light using the usual breathing method.

- *Sit on a hard-backed chair in front of all the crystals which are laid out together facing towards you, or if this is not possible due to their size, facing upwards. Sit as close to them as possible.*

- *Leave yourself open to receive the vibrations from these crystals for a few minutes.*

- *Commence whichever meditation exercise you wish to perform with the added assistance of the enhanced vibrations generated by the crystals.*

- *By only using these crystals for this purpose, they will continually gather the beneficial radiations produced during your meditations, as well as acting as enhancers. A virtuous circle will be created in which they both radiate and re-charge themselves during spiritual exercises, providing they are reserved for this use only, and are treated with care and respect.*

Crystals have their own natural life force, which naturally attracts a certain type of energy. This, combined with the procedures described above, is a helpful way of enhancing atmospheric conditions and is increasingly used nowadays.

⤳ READING CRYSTALS AND GEMS

Psychometry is the ability to psychically tune into objects and give readings based upon the information gained. No object is easier to do this with than precious metals and gemstones, which is why psychometrists so often work with rings, watches and necklaces. The wearer of these objects has unconsciously impressed their thoughts and feelings into the objects they wear, and experts can demonstrate staggering accuracy when reading them. And not only experts; I have run dozens of workshops in which complete novices have amazed themselves by discovering details about a complete stranger by psychometrising their ring or watch. They have been able to tell them what their house looks like in detail, what type of work they do, and details of their family, without any clues or other source of information. In doing so they have gained more proof that anyone can unlock their psychic powers than years of academic study at any university would give them. The best type of proof is personal experience.

Some believe that this principle was directly used by mystics to store specific information, which could only be realised by someone who was capable of practising advanced psychometry. According to some sources the philosopher's stone was a crystal device which was programmed with information. If the mystic who tried to penetrate its secrets was not clairvoyant enough, he or she would be unable to learn its secrets. Thus those who were not ready would be naturally prevented by their lack of advancement from discovering secrets which they were not meant to learn. It was an automatic filter based on psychic ability.

Crystals hold the key to a new science, often termed radionics, which new-age thinkers see as the next great step. Already pioneers like Dr King have worked with it to store and tap sources of spiritual energy. Perhaps in the future it will be recognised that it is potentially as important as was the advent of electronics. But let's not wait until then.

KEY 12

Tuning into Music

MUSIC HAS LONG BEEN associated with the elevation of the spirit. Devotees of Wagner, for example, sometimes talk about his music as though it were a religious experience, and for them maybe it is. Certain types of music induce a sublime state of consciousness, akin to a meditative state, others cause a highly charged, emotional response. There is no doubt that certain types of music are conducive to enhance meditation, and that meditation itself can aid the composition and performance of some music, because it creates openness and receptiveness in the musician.

Recent research by scientists in the US has shown that the region of the brain responsible for posture, balance, co-ordination and fine motor movements is larger in classically trained male musicians than in men who do not play a musical instrument. Speaking at the 1998 annual meeting of the American Society for Neuroscience, Dr Gottfried Schlaug, of Boston's Beth Israel Deaconess Medical Center, said researchers had used a brain scan to compare the brains of 32 right-handed musicians with 24 right-handed nonmusicians. Their results showed that the cerebellums of the musicians were five per cent bigger than those of the nonmusicians. Interestingly, these findings did not apply to a smaller survey of women, which may be because they tend to be more intuitive anyway.

Some scientists are re-discovering the ancient idea of music as a form of healing, so prevalent in early Greek culture. They postulate that since rhythm, harmony and melody stimulate several areas of the brain, they could be used to help repair everything from damaged speech to damaged emotions. Already doctors use a technique called melodic intonation therapy to teach stroke patients to sing rather than speak what they want to convey, and in some cases they can recover their speech. Anne Blood of the Montreal Neurological Institute and McGill University in Canada, examined emotional responses to music among people with untrained ears. Brain scans showed different regions of the brain responded both to harmony and discord, in other words music seems to switch on brain regions not normally used. She intends this research to reveal how different types of music can help cure different kinds of neurological disorder. Encouraging as this research is, many of us did not need to be told that music can be used for healing. It is, after all, only a means of transmitting energy through sound.

❧ THE ELEMENTS OF MUSIC

According to Eastern mystics the first element in creation was ether, which is associated with the sense of sound; and in the Bible, the Word came first, which presumably manifested itself in sound. Of all the art forms on earth, music is the most popular – there are very few people who do not listen to one form of music or another. Compared with the visual arts, music has had far more effort, money and time devoted to it over a longer period, and is arguably the most evolved art form. It is used in all cultures to evoke every kind of emotion, including love, aggression, peace, turbulence, joy, depression and more. And this is the point really. Music, however skilfully produced, is not necessarily a good thing. It is only as good as the reactions it creates in others.

My background is in music of all kinds. I have played several instruments and/or sung in everything from orchestras to rock bands to jazz combos to country and western groups to classical ensembles to cathedral choirs. Most recently I produced an album called *Mindfield* with a brilliant young musician called Basil Simonenko, which includes techno, rapping and new-age music. Music can be used purely for entertainment; it can also touch the soul. You do not need to be trained in music for this to happen. I have also met professional musicians who have become blasé through familiarity and have lost their enthusiasm through regarding it too much as a living and not sufficiently as a love. Others never lose their initial passion. I found myself that the process of analysing Haydn, Mozart and Beethoven symphonies at university more for their structure than their beauty deadened my appreciation of these composers for a while. The intellectual left-hand side of the brain was coming into play automatically, as I was trained, and my natural, intuitive responses were being blocked out.

Music, like life itself, can be broken down into five major elements, which are as follows.

- **Melody** This is the main line of music which the mind is following, sometimes referred to as the pitch. These can be short phrases or long tunes, and they are usually deliberately designed to be memorable.

- **Harmony** This is the combination of all the notes of music being played simultaneously, sometimes referred to as density. It can include a combination of melodies (counterpoint) or the same melody being played at different times by different instruments (fugue). Some modern forms of music encourage discordant harmonies, but I believe this is a contradiction in terms, which defies the natural laws of harmony.

• **Quality** Traditionally this would simply be choosing which musical instrument to use when, and how to combine them. With the advent of electronics, it is increasingly about electrically generated sounds, some of which imitate known instruments and others which are original. This element is sometimes referred to as timbre. It also includes the way instruments are played, e.g. with or without vibrato.

• **Rhythm** This can be complex or simple. In most classical music, rhythms are simple times such as 2/4, 3/4, or 4/4. Occasionally composers explore beyond these, especially twentieth-century composers such as Stravinsky. However, the biggest advances came from the general discovery and acceptance of indigenous music from Africa, South America and other parts of the world, initially in jazz and then in blues and modern forms of music.

• **Volume** This is simply the degree of noise output, which adds light and shade. In a solo piano piece this is absolutely critical, while in a rock concert it can be almost negligible, since there is a constant level of sound with only occasional exceptions.

By using these five elements, feeling is introduced into music, and this feeling generates a response in the listener of one kind or another. Conditioning also plays a part. It is a rare person who can sit down and listen to a completely new form of music and immediately understand what it is all about. The first time I heard some drum and bass dance music, for example, I found it bland and repetitive; there was no discernible melody other than a constantly repeated short phrase, the harmony was uninteresting and the volume unchanging. Without much variety or evolution of melody, harmony and volume, there seemed little else of interest. Then my nephew explained to me that it was mainly about quality and rhythm. It was not so much about memorable tunes as exciting new sounds which had been electronically created, and a complex blend of subtle rhythm changes. It was then no longer bland, but adventurous. Similarly, a lover of violin music might thrill to a solo performance of Paganini exercises (which would be boring to many people), because he would know all the nuances of the virtuosity being displayed and would appreciate the subtlety of the sounds being created.

These examples show that it is necessary to detach from what the mind is used to in order to tune into the essence of music. Just as the first step in meditation is to observe the tape loops of habit and see things anew, so with music it is important not to be conditioned by habitual tastes to get to the core of the energy contained within all music regardless of its genre.

❧ Mysticism in music

In ancient Greece music was equated with mathematics and astronomy. The composition of music is, in many ways, a mathematical procedure, relying on numerical divisions of various kinds to create harmonic structures. To the Greeks, these were the scales (Ionian, Doric and so on), upon which different musical pieces were based. In Western classical music, the twelve-note scale is the basis of all musical composition. Indian music explores more minute divisions than this, such as quarter tones, as does some jazz and rock and roll, in which instruments like the trombone and electric guitar are able to slide through notes, just slightly moving them through the divisions between the notes for various effects. On the whole, though, it is the twelve-note scale (the black and white notes on a piano between each octave) which is the basis of most music in history.

To the mystic, this fact is not just mathematical but also numerological in its significance. Numerology is to mathematics what astrology is to astronomy. It does not just deal with the facts about numbers and formulae connected with them, but draws mystical conclusions from them as well, just as an astrologer does from the position of various planets in your chart. For example the number 'one' may be taken by a numerologist to denote leadership, isolation or ego; the number 'two' communication, co-operation or relationships, and so on. The same principle can be applied to music. Pythagoras, a master of music as well as numbers, reputedly taught his students secret codes which unravel the meanings behind musical notes and the intervals between them. It is not by chance that there are the same number of notes as there are signs of the zodiac.

A closer examination of the numerical significance of the musical scale breaks it down still further. Although there are twelve actual notes, they fall into seven categories: A, B, C, D, E, F and G. After that we return to A. Seven is one of the most spiritually significant of all numbers, which is why it is referred to frequently in the Bible. Within these seven notes, there are always two opposing ones, the yin and yang of music if you like. These are generally referred to as the tonic and the dominant. There is an interval of a fifth between them, so that the dominant of C is G and the dominant of F is C. And within those relationships of tonics and dominants lies the harmonic and melodic key to all music. Using the chords C, F and G, for example, you can create a symphony or a twelve-bar blues. Naturally, they can be enhanced, modulated and developed, but they are the structural basis of nearly all types of music. They follow simple, numerical laws which, to the mystic, were placed there by the hand of God.

Perhaps that is why so much music has induced sublime or even religious experiences.

⟫ MUSIC AND MEDITATION

Music is a very immediate art form. It confronts you directly with sound in a way that art does not do with light. Literature is indirect, in that you need to use your intellect and imagination just to absorb it. Even though I have put words to music, there is no doubt that opera and song limit the direct power of music; while the focus of attention is on the meaning of words, the power of the sound is diminished in its effect. The best way to absorb music is in a state of meditation, because then your mental barriers will be down, you will not be focused on its structural aspects, and you can take in the full impact.

There are two ways of combining music and meditation, and you need to be clear which of these you wish to achieve. The first is to use music as an aid to meditation. If you want to do this, you need music with little movement in it. The deeper you wish to go in meditation the less demanding you want the music to be, as can be seen from the following three-stage guide.

- **Imagination** Use this as an aid to specific visualisations and positive thinking practices. The music should be abstract, but with some elements to concentrate upon in order to occupy the mind and take it away from other extraneous thoughts.

- **Intuition** Use this as an aid to becoming more receptive and receiving thoughts emanating from outside sources. The music should be more abstract, but with a definite mood which induces peace and harmony.

- **Inspiration** This is a more active state, but the knowledge is coming from within you so you want very little to distract you. The music should create stillness and balance as a platform from which you can mentally soar to the heights.

The selection of suitable music to bring about the above reactions is a very personal choice. It is like choosing a method of divination from say the *I Ching*, the tarot pack, the crystal ball and the runes; the system you love is going to be the one which works best for you. This is also true of music, providing you know why you are selecting it and what you want to achieve. It is not a question of whether it impresses you, but how it affects you. Mahler, for example, was one of the most accomplished composers of all times, who wrote extremely powerful music. Undoubtedly, though, some of his music is melancholic and therefore not uplifting for some listeners. On the other hand, if you were already melancholic, it might be easy for you to relate to and therefore comforting.

An experiment into the effects of music upon plant growth published in Brett I. Bolton's *The Secret Power of Plants* indicated consistent results. Between 1968 and 1971, inside controlled environmental chambers at the liberal arts Temple Buell College in Denver, flowers were fed a daily diet of different types of recorded music. The flowers were placed in white plastic cups containing the same kind of soil, with light, temperature and air regulated automatically to ensure the same conditions for all. They were divided into three groups, one being exposed to rock and roll, the second to semi-classical music and hymns, with the sound volume the same for both groups. The third group (the 'control group') did not receive sound. In the first week, the petunias exposed to rock and roll did not bloom, but those exposed to semi-classical music gave six buds. After two weeks, the 'rock and roll plants' were leaning away from the radio and showing erratic growth, while the second set were leaning towards the speaker. The soothing music produced zinnias an inch and a half higher than those subjected to the rock music. Within a month the rock and roll group collapsed and died. Further tests showed that sitar music, Bach compositions and hymns brought greater growth, while loud and dissonant sounds brought wilting and death. The control group, which had not been subjected to any sound, did better than the rock and roll group on the whole, but not as well as the semi-classical group. In one test only the control group did better than both.

What you do *not* want in meditation is an active intellect, because you are trying to go beyond that. Therefore you do not want complexity in your music or an abundance of change in any of the five elements listed on pages 114–115. A repetitive tune, for example, will tend to distract your concentration from the focus of your meditation, as will a catchy rhythm or an exciting variety of sounds. It is very difficult for a composer who is used to music as a medium of entertainment, and has to constantly catch the listener's attention, to write for meditation, which is attempting to achieve the exact opposite. This music is a creator of moods and a foil for distraction, but should never become an attention-grabber in its own right. Since around the late 1970s, new-age music has been specifically devised as an aid to the meditative and healing process; it is generally completely harmonious and calm with soothing rhythms.

The second method of combining music and meditation is to use the meditation as a way of absorbing more of the music at a deeper, intuitive level than you would normally do. You become one, not just with the sounds, but with the feeling and energy behind them.

MEDITATION ON MUSIC

- *Prepare yourself as usual with some deep and even breathing.*

- *Put on the music you have selected, but instead of listening in the normal way, let it wash over you as though you were having a sound bath.*

- *Avoid following any of the five elements specifically; just accept the whole at an energy level. Try to feel it entering you.*

- *You can enhance this by literally breathing in the music from the speakers of your sound system on the in-breath, and on the out-breath try to feel the effect of what you have breathed in.*

- *The purpose of this exercise is not to follow every note or phrase, but to get a general sense of the music as a whole. It does not matter if you miss bits, just absorb it in doses to conform with your breathing patterns.*

- *Feel as though you are floating in a sea of music, that it is a part of you and it travels right through you as water appears to do when you bathe.*

Music is not just the food of love; it can be the food of any emotion. It can stimulate aggression in a 'punk rock' concert or peaceful feelings at an Indian sitar recital. And it is not just the nature of the music which does this, it is the way it is used. Many have been elevated to spiritual heights by the orchestral music of Wagner, and yet the same music was used by the Nazis. After all, black and white magicians use the same energy, but for very different purposes.

If you tune into music and tap its inner power, you will be able to use it to enhance not only your meditations, but whatever spiritual goal you determine.

KEY 13

Seeing the Future

TIME PASSED SLOWLY; the day went in a flash –
two apparently meaningless statements. After
all, time moves at a fixed rate, which we measure
on our clocks. But how accurate *is* our measurement of time
when our thoughts and feelings see it differently. An hour can
take forever if we are waiting to hear important news, and
virtually disappear if we are enjoying what we are doing. Is
our perception really less accurate than hours, minutes and
seconds? Vast experience can be gained in a few hours, and
weeks can be wasted. Surely the amount and quality of experience is a more valid measurement than the calendar year.

As scientists start to grapple seriously with the concept of
time travel, many of the former certainties of rational science
are being thrown up in the air. Speeds faster than light are
being postulated, and the existence of invisible matter
suggests such massive gravitational forces that, under certain
conditions, travelling from one end of the galaxy to the other
could virtually happen instantaneously. Ideas which used to

be exclusively reserved for science-fiction are now being studied in university departments. So let me start this chapter with a prediction: the science of the new millennium will have to deal not only with the relationship between space and time, but the relationship between space, time and mind.

❧ PREDICTION

I have run dozens of classes and workshops designed to help people unlock their psychic powers. There are many techniques which will help them to do this, but the first step is always to alter your state of consciousness from the day-to-day mental processes into a more contemplative state of mind. Meditation is crucial in this process. According to mystics, if you know two of the three times – past, present and future – you automatically know the third; it is all a question of attunement. At any moment, there is a predictable future within certain parameters. This future can be plucked out of the mindfield around by someone who is sufficiently aware. Sometimes this is done unwittingly, as in the following amazing example. Fourteen years before the *Titanic* embarked on her maiden voyage from Southampton to New York in April of 1912, a novel was published called *Futility* by Morgan Robertson. This was about an apparently unsinkable ocean liner which, like the *Titanic*, was triple-screw and could make 24–25 knots. It was a little shorter than the *Titanic* at 800 feet, with a displacement of 70,000 tons (4,000 tons greater). Like the *Titanic*, it had a fashionable and glamorous passenger list and there were not enough lifeboats. On a night in April, this vessel struck an iceberg and sank to the bottom of the Atlantic. Its fictional name was Titan. Was this an amazing coincidence, or did Morgan Robertson, when imagining her plot, tune into the mindfield around her and unwittingly read a future event? Did H.G. Wells pick up on the future when he wrote in *The World Set Free* in 1914 about a weapon called 'an atomic bomb'?

This ability to see future events not only applies in

literature, but also in science. What made Aristarchus of Samos so certain that planets revolved around the sun 1,800 years before this fact was discovered by Copernicus? He had no firm evidence, and it was a theory which flew in the face of the established orthodoxy of the day – that the universe was centred on the earth. And how did an emperor of China, Hwang Ti, in around 3650 BC know that, as he noted, 'all the blood in the body is under the control of the heart ... the blood current flows continuously in a circle and never stops'. It was not until 1616 that William Harvey's experimental data confirmed that the heart functions as a pump and blood circulates throughout the body. These are not exactly predictions, but they do indicate an intuitive ability to recognise the truth centuries before it is proven.

Every culture has contained some form of divination; prophets, oracles and seers have always existed, just as they do today. Technological advances have not dampened people's appetite for knowledge of the future from practitioners in the art of divining. From China comes the I Ching; the tarot probably originated in Egypt; astrology now popular all over the world has its roots in Eastern countries; the runes come from Scandinavia; numerology has existed in many forms, but has many associations with the kabbalistic philosophy of the Middle East, and so on. I maintain that there is no end to the possible systems which could be devised for divination – that you could even give an accurate reading from watching car number plates if you were sufficiently in tune. No matter what system you use, you still need a degree of intuition to interpret your findings correctly.

The systems themselves follow the principle that nothing happens by chance. The runes, cards, lines on the palm of your hand, or whatever you are using, fall into a certain pattern. This pattern is not haphazard. In the case of astrology, a chart is based upon the exact position of all the planets in the solar system in relation to the place, date and time of your birth. Exhaustive study of data has been done into astrology by European research organisations such as the Institut für Demoskopie in Allensbach, Germany, and Gunter Sachs' 'Institute for Empirical and Mathematical Research into the Truthfulness of Astrology, concerning Human Behaviour and Predisposition' working with the Institute of Statistics at Munich's Ludwig-Maximilian University. They have shown that there are consistent patterns of behaviour in different star signs which defy chance. But even with a complex system like astrology, you need more to really see the future in detail. You need an instinctive feel for it. You need to tap your higher senses.

There is an inherent paradox in seeing the future. What is the point of knowing what is going to happen when you surely cannot alter it, because if you could alter it, it would not really be predictable. How can you prophesy something which might change? As with all metaphysical thinking, you need to think intuitively, beyond apparently contradictory intellectual statements. In fact, you can predict the future and you can alter it; both avenues are possible. At any moment in time you have a future, which with the ability of divination can be seen. You can then set about changing that future. If you could not, there would be absolutely no point in knowing it. A premonition is given to you to do something about it. We all mould our destinies 24 hours a day (including when we are asleep). The purpose of many of the biblical prophecies, for example, was to warn against dire events to come, so that, if possible, they could be avoided, or if they were not avoided, people would at least be better prepared to deal with them. The same is true of a personal prediction, which is designed to help you to capitalise on the benign aspects of your destiny and to minimise the negative aspects.

⤳ VISION

We all need vision in order to have some idea of where we are going and why; the vital thing is to make this vision feasible.

There is a self-fulfilling aspect to prediction. If you are told by a psychic that you will travel or change jobs next year, and you have faith in that psychic, you are more likely to make it happen. But it can also work the other way. One of the most frustrating calls I have ever received on a radio phone-in was from a lady who had been told, in a séance, the surname of the man she would marry. It was a long foreign name which she had never heard before, and she was given its exact spelling. Some years later she met a man of that name and fell in love with him. He asked her to marry him, but because she did not want to accept the findings of a séance, she turned him down and has lived to regret it ever since. This surely comes under the category of being downright awkward! On the other hand, there are those who go to psychics and hang on their every word. They try to make their predictions happen. There is a world of difference between correct psychic advice and fortune-telling. You do have to be careful in this area – there are charlatans and deluded practitioners as well as excellent, genuine ones. But even if you get first rate psychic advice, it is always a good thing to run it by your own intuition. Navigational advice is welcome, but you are still captain of your own ship.

Many methods are taught for developing clairvoyance, some much quicker than others. However, it is crucial that from the beginning you are in control of the whole procedure and can switch it on and off like a tap. If you ever feel you are losing the ability to maintain this essential element of self-control, stop the practice until you are able to do so again.

SECOND SIGHT MEDITATION

- *Darken the room so that it is only dimly lit.*

- *Start to observe the processes of your mind. Do not let your mind go blank, but distance yourself from everyday thoughts and allow them to dissolve until you enter a more meditative state. Only then, start the following practice.*

- *Use a transparent object such as a clear crystal or a bowl of still water in a glass dish. The first would be gazing, the second scrying, but the principle is exactly the same in both: to look at something so clear that it frees your mind to 'see' beyond the physical.*

- *Take a few deep breaths and then start looking at the crystal or water. Allow the eyes to go slightly blurred, which they will do naturally, but carry on looking through them. Do not let the mind go blank or enter any kind of trance. Remain alert but relaxed, just looking through the eyes into the empty space of the water or crystal.*

- *With practice, you may start to get at first a blurring, perhaps a smoky haze, and then one or more images. You need to differentiate between your imagination and a genuine psychic vision. At first you will not know which is which, so just keep an open mind, remain in control at all times and note what you see.*

- *If a scene unfolds as though it was a dream, remember it. It may be symbolic or real, and it could be about the future.*

- *When you decide to finish, it is important that you switch off at the end of the exercise by again focusing your eyes clearly on the physical objects in front of you.*

- *Take a few deep and even breaths to bring an element of control to the practice before you finish.*

This exercise can awaken faculties other than seeing the future. You might for example see what appears to be the face of someone you know to be dead. Ignore this if it happens. There are specific procedures for contacting guides, which are covered in Key Nineteen. It is vital in self-development to stick to the goal you have set, unless you are receiving personal instruction in the presence of an expert. It is always good to turn back to 'A Workout for the Mind' and remind yourself of the vital importance of concentration at all times. Uncontrolled psychics have lost the ability to concentrate on a specified goal and tend to wander mentally from one thing to another. If you avoid this from the very beginning, you can make sure it never happens to you. The previous exercise is fairly advanced and will not work for everyone, especially immediately. You will find that some psychic practices work better for you than others. If you draw a blank on this exercise, do not worry; you may find that in the future you will come back to it and get superb results. But whatever results you get, always remember the crucial aspect of interpretation: even if you see death, it cannot necessarily be taken literally and may represent a coming change. There will be some things you will not be able to explain immediately. Just keep an open mind. Keep them as memories in your mental filing system, and there may come a time when you suddenly click and the meaning is literally as clear as crystal.

KEY 14

Communicating With Animals

E VERYONE HAS A SPECIAL relationship with
their pet, but few people realise just how aware
animals can be in their own distinctive ways.
They have a different type of mental process to the human
mind, but it is translatable into human types of thought. Some
psychics specialise in communicating with animals and are
able to pick up from them details about the family they live
with, their house, garden and so on. Domestic animals are
very prone to habit-forming, and can be upset if their routine
is changed. They expect a certain amount of appreciation
and, strange as it may sound, like to be consulted; it is just
that their idea of consultation is very different from ours. We
have a responsibility to try to understand them since we have
domesticated them and they are dependent upon us. They are
attracted to a meditative environment. If you have pets, you
may have noticed that they tend to keep away when intense
discussions, particularly heated ones, are going on. When the
atmosphere is calm and reflective they are more likely to be

around you. It is this more meditative atmosphere which is one of the keys to gaining a deeper rapport with them; the others are a real love for them and a willingness to understand their point of view.

➤ ANIMAL TELEPATHY

There is a difference between animals who spend most of their time in your home and those who do not. If they do, you have to accept that they are just as much residents as you are, at least that is how they will see it. One of our cats actually regards himself as more of a resident than my wife and myself. After all, we go out every day and sometimes in the evening. The least we can do when we come back is to thank him for looking after the place in our absence. He made it clear to me that he felt that way one day when he started to become difficult and uncooperative, stopped using the cat litter and so on. His explanation was that his role in the home was not getting the recognition it deserved. After that, I started to thank him for looking after the house when I came home in the evening. He then became far more co-operative and started using the litter again.

I realise this may sound ridiculous, but there are dozens of similar stories, some far more complex than this one. One animal psychic, for example, was called in to help a racehorse who was refusing to race. After communicating with it, the psychic ascertained that the horse would normally have a rest period before racing, but this year had not been given one. She asked the owner whether this was true, and indeed it was. She then informed the horse that if it ran this one race, it would then definitely get a rest period. The horse ran the race, and sure enough it got its rest period afterwards. There are too many examples of psychic communication with animals leading to a positive change of behaviour in both the owner and the animal, to ignore it.

Most animal psychics communicate in pictures. Obviously,

animals do not think in words as we do, so if you wish to send them thoughts you have to send images. Nor do they have a sense of time as we do, only of routine. For example, if you want to say something which relates to early in the day, they will probably associate it with their first meal. So you visualise their first meal, and then the thing you are trying to tell them. If you are going on a journey, it is only fair to let them know rather than just letting them discover that you are not there. They may know the relevance of your suitcase, in which case visualise it being packed. Then mentally go through the number of meals they will have in your absence, which gives them some idea of the length of time you will be away. Then visualise your suitcase being unpacked. They will be far less unhappy when you go if you have at least prepared them and they have some idea of the timing of your return.

Many people talk to their pets and swear blind that the pets understand them. Quite possibly they do; it will not be the words, of course, but the feelings behind the thoughts which they pick up. In fact, animals can be better at picking up your feelings than some humans. There are numerous cases of animals who have known when their owner was grieving and tried to comfort them. If you greet your dog, cat or other animal with a 'Hello, how are you?' for example, of course they do not know intellectually what these words mean. But they will pick up that you are acknowledging them; you are not just taking them for granted as you walk into the house, which they loathe. They will know how pleased you are to see them by the tone in your voice and, even more, the vibrations you are emitting which they can often pick up instantaneously.

Animals are extremely sensitive to healing, both giving it and receiving it. If you are not well, they will sometimes come and lie on you or lick you better. One of the most famous cases of this is the legend of Saint Rock's dog. Saint Rock was a controversial monk who healed victims of the plague in Europe in the Middle Ages. Eventually he caught the plague himself while healing in Italy, and went to a forest to die so that nobody would catch it from him. A dog found him and decided to heal him, as the monk had done to so many others. He licked his wounds, fed him by bringing him food from the nearby town, and Saint Rock was eventually healed. He then went off with the dog and continued his healing work until the Vatican, upset by his work, imprisoned him on a spurious charge of spying. Centuries later he was canonised as the patron saint of healing the plague, and is now revered by the Catholic Church. Ironically, although they have come to terms with Saint Rock's work, they have still not recognised that animals have souls or even feel pain. Yet without that legendary dog, Saint Rock would not have been able to continue the healing work for which he was later canonised.

The charity, Pets as Therapy, initiated and carried out a two-part survey at Crufts Dog Show at the National Exhibition Centre in 1994 and 1995. Two hundred and ninety-one people took part in the 1994 study and 167 in 1995, giving an overall total of 458. All were given a blood pressure check by a nurse. Dog owners on average exhibited a slightly lower blood pressure reading (123/79) than those who did not possess a dog (134/85). Ninety-nine per cent of dog owners believed that owning a dog had improved the quality of their life. Over 50 per cent believed that they had been made ill through contact with other humans, and only 1 per cent that they had suffered illness in the last two years through contact with dogs. In 1992 the results of a three-year study of 5,741 people attending a risk-evaluation clinic in Australia provided proof that pets are good for your health, although the study had originally set out to prove the reverse. It was carried out by Dr Warwick Anderson at the Baker Medical Research Institute. Dietary habits, age, exercise, family history of heart disease, smoking and alcohol intake were all taken into account. Blood pressure, cholesterol levels and blood triglyceride were also examined. The results, published in *The Medical Journal of Australia* volume 157, 7

September, 1992, showed that pets are beneficial to humans from a health point of view.

Some people dispute whether animals feel pain at all – of course they do, just ask them. The whole debate about hunting and whether hunted animals feel any stress from the chase is absurd to anyone remotely psychic. Because they are so instinctive about life and death, in some ways they feel it more than some humans would. They also have souls and continue into the afterlife. I and many others have been able to describe to the owners of deceased animals exactly what the animals look like, because often they are still around them – pets are, after all, exceptionally loyal. They also recognise immediately when you are giving them healing, which you can easily do using the following meditation.

HEALING ANIMALS

- *Breathe deeply and evenly for a few moments, entering a meditative frame of mind.*

- *Place your hands upon the injured part of the animal. If this is not possible, place them on the back of the animal – the energy will still reach the affected area.*

- *Visualise white light coming down through you and into the animal, particularly on the out-breath. You may find that the animal's breathing pattern starts to change and lengthen, although it will probably be more shallow than yours.*

- *Try to be as calm as possible. Do not convey any of your worry or concern about the animal's health to it, because that will only worry it more. Just as animals are often a source of calmness for us humans when we have anxieties, it is for us to radiate calmness and peace to the animals when they are suffering.*

- *When you have finished, wash your hands and if necessary your garments. It is always best to perform healing wearing a white cotton coat, but this is not always possible with animals, especially if they are outside or dirty.*

- *The animal will probably know what you are doing, and be very receptive to receiving healing from you.*

➤ PSYCHIC ANIMALS

One of the most positive and dramatic examples of an animal demonstrating ESP (extrasensory perception) is a story from the First World War, told by one J.P.J. Chapman many years later. He was a mechanic in an Air Squadron in late October of 1918. The Germans were in retreat, and he was sent to an advance emergency landing ground with about 24 others and a hungry mongrel called Snuffer, who spent most of his time in the rough tin shack they used as a cookhouse. One day Chapman was assisting the cook, when Snuffer took Chapman's hand in his mouth and tried to lead him away. The dog was so insistent that they both followed him to a shell hole about 25 yards away. The cook wanted to go back to the cookhouse, but when he started to move, Snuffer growled fiercely until he changed his mind. It was not long before they heard a whine and then a terrible crash – the cookhouse had received a direct hit. For the rest of his life, Chapman was adamant that their lives had been saved by the premonition of a dog.

Animals also seem to remain instinctively loyal to their owner after death. A case was reported in Kilda, near Melbourne, Australia about a cat named Felix. Its owner died and the cat could not be comforted. To distract it, the family took Felix for a drive in the car. At the outskirts of Melbourne, the car stopped at a traffic light; Felix jumped out of an open window and could not be found. Ten days later the family went to the cemetery to visit the grave of Felix's former owner and found Felix pacing backwards and forwards on the grave. This cemetery was ten miles from their home and five miles from where the car had stopped at a traffic light. Another extraordinary report concerned a swarm of bees which seemed to have a group soul. John Zepkā of Adams, Massachusetts was an expert on beekeeping. In May 1956 he died and, according to reports, when his funeral cortege reached the grave, mourners found the tent and floral sprays swarming with bees. The bees remained immobile during the ceremony and then flew away. It was as though they were paying respect to someone who had spent so much of his life with them.

There are many more basic examples, such as when you arrive home unexpectedly early and your pet is waiting for you at the window, as if they knew you were coming. Perhaps they picked up your thoughts, or were able to psychically see what was going to happen. The following exercise will help you to establish a rapport with your animal.

ANIMAL RAPPORT

- *Have physical contact with the animal in question. It may be on your lap, or you may simply be touching it.*

- *Observe images and thoughts as they come to you, as though your brain were a radio receiver set.*

- *Also observe what you feel from the animal. It may be peaceful, upset or anxious for example.*

- *You may receive sentences, which will be your brain translating the abstract thoughts and feelings of the animal.*

- *If you get any particular idea, try communicating an answer by visualising it in picture form rather than in words.*

- *See what effect, if any, this has on the animal.*

- *If there are no problems in the animal's psyche, it may be that you both start to enter a meditative state together, which can be very beneficial to both of you. According to Buddhist writings, the Lord Buddha first entered enlightenment in the presence only of a cat.*

You may or may not achieve results from this practice. Some people have a far more natural rapport with animals than others. If you think you are getting something and have communicated back, see what results it brings. You may be able to help put something right which has been troubling the animal, for example, and if so its behaviour will change afterwards. Gradually you will find it easier and easier to know what is going on in their minds, which they will greatly appreciate!

THE THIRD EYE

Keys of Inspiration

KEY 15

Ecstasy Without Drugs

TAKING DRUGS FOR recreational purposes is not a freak pastime indulged in by a small minority of the population. It is very common, particularly, but not exclusively, among young people. According to statistics compiled in Britain in 1998 over a three-month period, four per cent of those aged between 16 and 25 use the drug ecstasy, and the actual figure could be even higher than that. Cannabis is the most commonly used drug among 11 to 25 year olds, and there are many others. They are all dangerous, some far more than others, and none of them should be used.

I am not trying to write a sociological treatise here, but to provide an infinitely preferable alternative to drugs. The desire to get high is not in itself wrong, in fact it can be very right; only the method is wrong. For a start the effects of drugs are short-lived, usually only a matter of hours; secondly, they are damaging to the neuro-physical system to a greater or lesser degree depending on the drug; and above

all, they have addictive properties, mentally and/or physically, which can ruin your life. But the urge to transcend your
normal level of consciousness into something higher is
entirely natural. Too many people are doing it to dismiss
them all as psychologically flawed, or a product of a difficult
childhood. Some experts in Britain believe that the drug
ecstasy, for example, which tends to induce a feeling of
benign warmth to anyone you meet, is one of the main
factors which greatly reduced football violence in Britain in
the late 1980s. Under the influence of this drug young
people had no wish to be violent to each other. At the same
time, there have been tragic and fatal consequences from
taking the drug. What we need is the benign feelings, the
inspirational states, without the dangers brought on by
taking drugs.

⇒ BECOMING INSPIRED

Having tapped into the power of your imagination and the
guiding light of your intuition, the third step on the ladder of
personal evolution is the transmuting force of inspiration.
This is the force which changes the world. Imagination
awakens your mind to new possibilities; intuition enables you
to tap into information beyond yourself, which is not just
restricted to your brain but which is in the universal sea of
mind; inspiration is a combination of both these things and
more. It is the most productive use of your imagination,
coupled with the highest level of intuitive awareness. And yet
it is almost abstract in its nature. It is not just picking up
something which is already out there, but creating something
from nothing. It produces the greatest of inventions and the
most original works of arts. Imagination is thinking; intuition
is feeling; but inspiration, at its height, is knowing. It can
come in a flash, as if from nowhere, so much so that it can
look easy. But somewhere down the line inspired people have
worked and sweated to reach the state of realisation which

makes them inspired – hence the saying that a great work of accomplishment takes 99 per cent perspiration and 1 per cent inspiration.

The most inspired people in history are geniuses. They were not necessarily great intellectuals, they may or may not have had good memories and a high IQ, but they always had the ability to tap the force of inspiration. The great artist Turner, for example, with his sublime sensibilities expressed in delicate and refined paintings, was regarded by those who knew him as a coarse person, or as we say in England, a 'rough diamond'. Wagner, with his elevated works which appeal to the highest and most noble instincts within us, held political views which were nothing short of disgusting. An inspired genius who mastered all the basic aspects of his or her nature would move to an even higher level of awareness.

Inspiration is a force which needs to be controlled. If it is, there are no limits to what you can achieve, not so much for yourself, but for the world as a whole. It is inspiration which will eventually bring peace. Politicians can negotiate until they are blue in the face, but until the people they are negotiating for are inspired to change and drop their differences, there will not be a lasting peace. Inspiration will eventually end poverty. This is the force which causes a wealthy person to become a philanthropist, to reject the never-ending cycle of greed in favour of satisfying the urge to give to others. When you become inspired, you affect the mindfield around you permanently. The elevated thoughts and feelings you project travel through the ethers of space and others may pick them up. Even reading a book like this and thinking about these things will affect not only you, but to a greater or lesser extent the sea of mind around you. If everyone on earth decided simultaneously, just for a few minutes, to think positively about world peace, the world would permanently change because the mind waves generated would transmute much of the negativity which is out there. That alone is a good reason to become inspired.

⤳ A NATURAL HIGH

Apart from the dangers involved, there is a key difference
between a drug-induced high and a natural high. In the
1960s, people who wanted to be 'groovy' ('cool' nowadays)
usually tried soft drugs at least. But some found that natural
methods were self-controlled and infinitely more rewarding.
When a drug-induced state ends, which is determined not by
you but by the substance you have used, you are back to
normal. You cannot regain it except by taking more drugs,
which may or may not give you the same state. After all, not
every drug-induced experience is a positive or pleasant one
by any means. In the case of a naturally induced high, the
realisation that you achieve is yours forever. Because you have
made the effort to bring it about, you do not lose it. You can
tap into its memory and it changes you permanently for the
better.

You can be miserable in a palace and joyful in a cave. Joy is
something you experience in your mind; it is not the result of
physical conditions. Physical conditions may inspire you of
course: a country walk, a beautiful mountain, a superb work of
art, the technological feat of an impressive car. But the reaction still takes place in the mind. If you are heart-broken,
these things will not impress you nearly so much as if you are
with your partner in the first flush of romance. Your state of
mind is all-important. I came to the conclusion that it would
be possible to induce states of ecstasy, and ran a workshop at
a festival just for this purpose. It was experimental, and I must
say I did not expect the results we got. There were people
who literally had tears of joy running down their cheeks.
There had been no physical changes to their lives; they were
sitting on hard-backed chairs in very ordinary surroundings
practising various forms of meditation. I should have realised
I suppose. Too many yogis have related incredible experiences while living isolated lives in the Himalayas or remote
forests to dispute the fact that it really is all in the mind.

Our reactions to events are determined by inner consciousness far more than the event itself. For example, when Princess Diana died there was mass mourning. When her sons, a year later, appealed to people to bring this to an end and allow them to deal with their mother's death in peace, Buckingham Palace received complaints from members of the public that the princes' request was interfering with their grieving process. This type of absurdity, not to mention insensitivity, had little to do with Princess Diana and a lot to do with their own states of mind. They wanted the opportunity to express their grief, so they virtually hijacked Princess Diana's death as an excuse to bring it out. This did not apply to everybody of course, but when a radio phone-in caller says that they felt worse about Princess Diana's death than they did when their own wife died of cancer, it is clear that there is a lot of denial going on. We did not see as many people sending flowers and lining the streets for peace in Northern Ireland, which was a more significant event in terms of saving lives. People were not willing to express their joy to the same extent that some were willing to express their grief. And yet the expression of joy does far more good to the mindfield, because it feeds it with positive energy, which others can then draw upon.

By cultivating a natural high you sow seeds of inspiration which will blossom in your life and affect the whole. The yogis who lived in caves were not selfish as they may have appeared; the greatest among them entered deep samadhic states to change the consciousness of the whole world for the better. But there is no need to go that far. You can cultivate positive and even ecstatic states of awareness without leaving your home. And it is far better to live in the world and become more directly involved in the process of raising world consciousness.

MIND-RAISING

- *Practise deep and even breathing.*

- *Increase the speed of your breaths while keeping them as deep as possible. Fill your lungs vigorously with more and more air, without causing any strain. If you have a weak heart, just breathe gently.*

- *If you experience any dizziness, stop the practice and rotate your head on the neck for a few moments until the dizziness passes.*

- *With practice, you should be able to build this up so that you feel invigorated and energised without dizziness. At this point, hold the breath in for as long as you can, again without any strain. Let the air out slowly.*

- *Now recall the happiest moment of your life, not as a nostalgic, sentimental experience, but to recall the joy and enlightenment you felt at the time.*

- *Suddenly detach from this and repeat the power breathing method, as before. When you feel sufficiently invigorated, hold the air in your lungs for as long as possible, then let it out slowly.*

- *Now quickly think of your favourite outdoor location in the world and imagine you are there completely alone. Use as many senses as possible as well as vision – smell the air, feel the warm or cool air, whichever you have chosen, and hear the sounds of birds singing or whatever it may be, depending upon your selected location.*

- *Suddenly detach from this and practise the power breathing method for a third time until you are invigorated. Your body may feel light, as though you could virtually take off. Hold the breath in for as long as possible and let it out slowly.*

- *Now visualise yourself seated in a pillar of pure white flame, which is gradually spreading through and around you.*

Although it is snow white, it is alive and pulsating, going way above your head and affecting all those around you. It burns, but it gives off no heat. If you do this properly, you should feel yourself tingling all over.

- *In the midst of this white pulsating light, stop visualising anything specific and see what comes to you immediately. It may be a thought; it may be the answer to something which has been concerning you for years; it may be a picture; it may be a vision. Or it may not be anything, in which case you may not need anything specific at the present time.*

- *Note whatever comes to you, but do not try to force anything. It will either happen or it won't – inspiration happens quickly or not at all.*

- *If you feel a warm sense of inner contentment, peace or joy, bathe in it for a few more moments, as though you were feeling the lower aspects of your mind with the higher ones.*

KEY 16

Making Your Own Luck

THERE IS NO SUCH thing as luck other than the luck you make yourself. It does not always look that way of course. People who live good and noble lives sometimes seem to be beset with misfortune, while others who behave dishonorably seem to land on their feet. But that is only in the space of one lifetime. Making your own luck has to be seen in the context of reincarnation, which will be explored in detail in Key Seventeen. There is a lot you can do to capitalise on your luck in this life.

✤ MEDITATION AND LUCK

An increasing amount of academic research is being carried out into luck and its causes. A recent American study isolated a type of mildly brain-damaged person who, despite good intelligence and memory, often fouls up in life. Scientists at the University of Iowa College of Medicine set up an experiment with two groups of patients who were given cards, some

of which awarded money and other penalties. The group of
patients with brain defects took longer to access the difference between the cards, and even after doing so still chose
the penalty cards. They had no hunch about which were
more fortunate. The college's research suggests that bad luck
may be biological and the possibility that unfortunate people
have a loser's lobe. Dr Richard Wiseman of the psychology
department at the University of Hertfordshire has undertaken
research into luck and intuition. He told the *Independent* news-
paper: 'Some people do seem to be exceptionally lucky;
others seem extremely unlucky. Their luck is not just manifest
in health and wealth; more random events also seem to go in
their favour.'

Whether luck is a biological or psychological phenomenon, it is affected by mental processes, which will be
enhanced through meditation. A meditative state will tend to
enhance your positive characteristics and reduce the negative
ones, therefore leading to greater good fortune. It will also
lead to a deeper understanding of the natural forces behind
destiny which are summarised in the ancient but increasingly
colloquial term, karma.

❧ MANIPULATING YOUR KARMA

Dr George King was a master practitioner of karmic manipu-
lation, and as his student I learnt many things at close
quarters about this science. If you read the Eastern writings
on karma, you are left with the impression that karma, the law
of cause and effect, is almost something negative which
happens to you when you do wrong and have to learn lessons.
This is indeed a totally negative way of looking at it. Karma is
a benign law designed to help you, not to punish you. Even
the difficult lessons purely exist as essential teachings; they
are steps you have to take before you can progress any further
in your evolutionary journey.

You should look at karma not so much as a mysterious force

beyond your control, as though it were virtually a superstitious thing, but as something natural and all-pervasive which you can harness in a positive way. Every positive seed you sow will blossom at some time in the future. Every time you help someone, you are that much more likely to be helped when you need to be. Whenever you give, you are that much more likely to receive. If you serve others, you will advance more, with fewer obstacles in your path. Tests will always come along – if they did not life would not be worth much. A life without challenge is soon forgotten – it is as though nothing happened. The memories which count are those of accomplishments of one kind or another. But manipulating karma will smooth life's passage and, even more importantly, help everyone you come into contact with at the same time. It is not easy, but it is simple. Complicated explanations are usually devised as a cover for philosophies which do not work. Manipulating karma *does* work. You help others and you help yourself simultaneously – there is no tension between these two things. There is no need to question motives because actions reveal all. Even if you started out down a path of service partly out of self-interest, that motive would soon be transmuted into one simple desire: to co-operate with a natural law which is itself designed to bring the greatest good. It becomes a rhythm in your life, because it is the rhythm of life.

MEDITATING ON KARMA

- *It is very beneficial to reflect meditatively on your own karmic pattern from time to time.*

- *Start by becoming calm, taking deep and even breaths.*

- *Run through some recent events which seem to have happened to you. They may be fortunate or unfortunate ones.*

- *Try to detach from any emotional feelings you have about them, and do not attempt to think them through during this*

exercise. Simply allow impressions and memories to throw
light on their purpose in your life.

- *If you are confused by anything which has happened to you,*
  throw out a mental request for an answer.

- *Allow the answer to come, either as an image or a form of*
  words, as though it was travelling through the space around
  you. In fact it will come from your own superconscious mind.

- *If you do not get an answer during this exercise, be patient.*
  The meditation has set a process in motion, and the answer
  may pop into your head later at some unexpected moment.

ꙮ SYNCHRONICITY

Jung developed the concept of synchronicity when he
realised that some events are too coincidental to be coincidences (another paradox). Let me give you an outstanding
example of this. The writer, Colin Wilson, discovered that,
but for a coincidence, the First World War may not have
happened. Archduke Franz Ferdinand of Austria was assassi-
nated at Sarajevo by a young Bosnian patriot, Gabriel Princip,
in June 1914. As a consequence, Austria declared war on
Serbia. It was then up to the Tsar of Russia to decide whether
to stand by Serbia and declare war on Austria or let the
Balkans solve their own problems. On two previous occasions, the Tsar had been dissuaded from going to war by his
adviser, the controversial mystic, Rasputin. It was therefore
critical that Rasputin would be on hand to advise him at that
point. Unfortunately, Rasputin had been stabbed by a would-
be assassin in his home village of Pokrovskoe and hovered
between life and death. The Tsar, without Rasputin's advice,
declared war, which led to the First World War. Wilson's
research revealed an extraordinary so-called coincidence:
Rasputin and the Archduke had been struck down at exactly
the same time. Rasputin's daughter gave the time of his stab-

bing as shortly after 2.00 p.m. on 27 June. The Archduke, who had a premonition he would die and had told his children's tutor before leaving for Sarajevo that: 'the bullet that will kill me is already on its way', was killed at 11.00 a.m. on the same day. Wilson's research showed that there are 50 degrees of longitude between Sarajevo and Pokrovskoe, so the time in the two places differs. A turn of 50 degrees takes exactly 3 hours and 20 minutes – the approximate difference in time between the two deaths. Thus the two people who could possibly have averted the First World War were struck down in unrelated incidents at virtually the same time.

Synchronicity happens all the time. Yesterday I had letters to send all over the world and needed some stamps. I did not know exactly what it would cost, so I bought £20 worth. The postal costs ranged from 20 pence to 63 pence, depending on where I was sending the letters, and yet when they were all added up they came to exactly £20. A trifling incident which means little or nothing, yet is an extremely odd coincidence. On the other hand, here is another strange incident from my life which, I believe, does mean something. In 1973 I became very interested in UFOs. I was at university on a small grant and could not afford to buy the books I wanted on UFOs as well as a pair of gym shoes to play squash in, so I chose the books. A few days later one of the biggest UFO sightings in Hull took place. It was a cigar-shaped object seen by dozens of people. A friend and I drove out to get a good view of it and reached a field. We walked across the field, which was wet as it had been raining, and observed the UFO moving slowly across the sky until it became obscured by a large oak tree. I looked down to the ground and there, under the oak tree, was a brand new pair of completely dry gym shoes, seemingly unused and my size. I looked up again and the UFO was in view for a few moments before it disappeared. This I took to be a sign – not that the gym shoes were directly connected with the UFO, but they were, I believe, life's way of showing me that UFOs would have a great significance to me in the future (which they have). The next time you have a synchronicity experience, do not ignore it – it may have a meaning for you. There is no finer method of divination than the signs provided by life itself.

⤳ FORTUNE

Good fortune is something you cultivate; there is a magic to it. Here are some universal guidelines to follow, which are in tune with natural law.

- Try to make everything you do helpful to others as well as yourself.

- When you make money, give some away to those whose need is greater than yours.

- Do not be possessive in relationships; never try to keep someone against their will. Let them be with you because they want to be.

- Be as positive as you can. If you have anything negative which you feel has to be said about anyone, always say it to their face.

- When you have to make a long journey, visualise a safe arrival at the other end before you depart.

- Go with the flow rather than being bound to a particular idea. Always be ready to change.

- When dealing with any kind of opposition to something you have to do, use truth as your weapon. Even if you are outspoken in your words and thoughts, try to keep love in your heart. This will deny opponents any ammunition against you.

These are not just well-meaning principles – they really work. A cynic would look at that list and laugh. They would not even try it, which is why they will never discover whether it works. Yet they are all old ideas found in several religious and philosophical systems. These systems were not originally devised just to be nice ideas. They were devised because they work in life – for you and everyone else.

Fortune is not something you tell; it is something you create every minute of every day and night. Thoughts are things, and sooner or later will reflect in your life. Some modern theories of psychology are erroneous from a karmic point of view, even though they may work psychologically in the short term. It is impossible to get something bad out of your system just by expressing it. Life is a balance between suppression and expression. Neither action on its own, is the answer. Suppression of bad energies only delays things, and can ultimately make them worse. Expression releases them but causes a negative karmic reaction because of the effect you have had on the mindfield through putting out this bad energy. The only answer to negative thoughts and emotions is positive ones. The more positive vibrations you put out, the more you get back. One can talk forever on this subject, write long treatises to add to the accumulating writings on the subject and hold lengthy discussions. But when all is said and done, it boils down to this simple fact: what you put out comes back to you for better or for worse, sooner or later. You are not lucky or unlucky – you are the architect of your own destiny.

KEY 17

Remembering Past Life Experiences

LOT OF NONSENSE IS spoken about past lives, most of it harmless, some of it not. The worst experience I encountered was at a major festival where I was due to speak. Another speaker, who was very popular at these events, was running a 'past life workshop', designed to take people back to their past lives in a bid to heal this one. I met a young man who had been ejected from this workshop for causing a disturbance. He was very distraught, so I tried to help. He had come to the conclusion, during one of the exercises in the workshop, that he had been a Nazi SS Officer during the last war and was consumed with guilt. He had broken down during the meeting – hence the disturbance and the ejection. I asked him how he came to that conclusion, and he told me that, during one of the visualisation exercises, he had seen images of concentration camps, Nazi uniforms and other associations with that terrible time. They came to him as if from nowhere, and that was proof enough for him. I advised him that just seeing images like this proves nothing – it could be in his imagination, or it could be a psychic impression. He was too distraught to concentrate, left the festival and by the time he came back a few days later, he was a born-again Christian warning against the dangers of festivals.

I know this is a strange way to start a chapter on past life experiences, which I fully believe in, but it is necessary to be very clear from the beginning that this is not a field for naive experimentation. Nor is it a field for any type of dogmatism. I am a massive fan of Tibetan Buddhism, but the idea that the Dalai Lama, or indeed any lama, always reincarnates in Tibet as a man with the same task, defies the logic of karma, which is designed to provide a soul with a whole variety of experiences: different countries, religions, sexes and social positions. Nor do people reincarnate as insects in one life, humans in the next, then a bird and so on. There is an evolutionary logic to reincarnation in order to provide continuity, to learn the essential lessons and to balance karma. Humans reincarnate as humans in all normal cases.

Nor should past life recall be regarded primarily as a therapy, even though it has helped many people. Past life regression, where a patient is taken back through hypnosis into a former life, has proved the case for reincarnation. When someone in a hypnotic trance is able to describe a historical scene which they had no way of knowing about from their experiences of this life, it cannot be ignored. And there are some wonderful stories of help given to people as a result. One of the most beautiful ones I heard concerned an autistic child in New York, who had the dangerous habit of walking into the street and trying to stop cars with his hands. Hypnotic regression took him back to a former life in which he had been a traffic cop, which he was still living out. Once this was identified as the cause of his dangerous behaviour, they were better able to work on curing him. The downside of seeing it mainly as a therapy is that you are liable to adopt a negative approach to the subject. The focus will be too much on removing pain, and not enough on capitalising on and developing the positive aspects of previous lives, which is what I will concentrate on in this Key.

⇒ THIS IS THE LIFE

Past life experiences are only useful if they relate directly to this life. The idea should not be to work out a list of characters from previous times that you think you might have been, as if you were compiling your own 'Who's Who'. It is very unlikely that you will know exactly who you were anyway, nor do you need to in most cases. One of the main reasons we cannot remember exactly who we were is to prevent us from mentally slipping back too much to that life and away from this one. Another reason is that it could be confusing and even traumatic. We are here now to live this life, and any past life experiences we remember are only there to throw light on this one. Anyone who tells you who you were in a past life, unless they are extremely advanced spiritually, is probably wrong. If they are right, they certainly do not understand the metaphysics of the subject or they would realise that this is something for you to remember only when you are ready to do so. Similarly, most people who do remember their past lives accurately choose not to share the information widely with others. They have been given the ability to remember it for their own use.

There are rare exceptions to this, which only serve to prove the rule. One of these was investigated by Dr Ian Stevenson, a professor at the University of Virginia Medical School. In 1966, he published a work entitled 'Twenty Cases Suggestive of Reincarnation', detailing examples from many cultures, including India, Turkey, Thailand, England, Canada and Alaska. One concerned an Indian man of about 50 who claimed to remember a former life as a British military officer in the First World War. He said that he had been killed in battle when a bullet pierced his throat. In this life he had twin birthmarks on each side of his throat which looked like bullet scars, though that was not offered as any kind of evidence. He remembered the name of the Scottish town he came from, some words and phrases from the local dialect of that town, the names of his parents and the location of his house. He described identifying features of the landscape and a hilltop outside the town containing the ruins of a church. Most of these details could not have been discovered by the Indian man from any other source, according to Dr Stevenson's research. Dr Stevenson flew to the town in Scotland named by this man and found it to be just as he had described, including words of the dialect, and the family names he had given.

Whenever you get a case like this, there are always cynics who want to disprove it. As with all things psychic and spiritual, the only lasting way to prove these things to yourself is through your own experience. More important than proof, the information is there to be used constructively in this life. In fact this life should be the starting point, not the other way round. Some people who feel they are leading an insignificant life now will try to compensate for this feeling by believing that they were some great person in the past. It is easy to dismiss this as total delusion, and in many cases it may be, but there is another possibility. If you get a flashback from a past life, it is much easier to connect it in your mind with a famous person. For example, you might get a mental flash of the House of Commons when Gladstone was Prime Minister. From this you might conclude that you were indeed Gladstone, or one of his ministers, when in fact you may have been one of the cleaners in Parliament. It is much easier for your brain to connect with the name Gladstone, whom you have heard of in this life, than with the cleaner whom you have not. Hence there are numerous William Tells, Queens of Sheba and Wyatt Earps walking around, and probably no bakers or hairdressers from the same periods. You might find some tell-tale clues about who you were in the past from the following pointers.

- Start by reviewing the things you knew about from childhood. Surveys have shown extreme cases of children who knew words from languages they had never been taught, and that their parents did not know. Look at more basic things, such as areas of natural talent – gifts that you did not need to learn, only to develop. What were your instinctive passions and interests? What did you know about without having to be taught?

- Are there any people you have met whom you instinctively knew immediately, not just in general terms, but their specific behaviour patterns? You had an instant rapport with them, and it was as though you were continuing an existing friendship or relationship rather than starting a new one.

- Are there any countries you have been to in which you instantly felt at home? You were familiar with their customs, language and even recognised places you visited as if you were returning there. My tutor at university told me that when he first visited Calcutta, he knew where some of the streets would lead and what would be round the corner. He became convinced of reincarnation through this experience.

- Have you had any thought patterns which do not seem to belong in this life? When I was a teenager, I was troubled by recurring thoughts which bore no relation to anything I was experiencing in this life. Later, when I became aware of a past life, they fitted in and I could see why these things would trouble me.

- Is there any period of history which seems familiar to you, so much so that you may even disagree with the way historians record it? After all, they can only base their theories on available data, which can be as reliable as certain tabloids in reporting facts. Margaret Thatcher's and Nigel Lawson's versions of some events and discussions are so different that they are unrecognisable, and this was only from the 1980s. How much more unreliable will records of distant times and places be from the scant data available, which will also be biased by the views of scribes.

These are some ways of identifying general past life experiences. It is not necessary to draw any firm conclusions from this, but it may give you a general picture which you can then build on. For example, if you loved the Lake District and wrote poems as a child, it does not mean you were Wordsworth, but it may throw some light on your potential as a writer which is an ability you could use in this life.

➤ SPECIFIC RECOLLECTIONS

Everything nowadays is blamed on your upbringing or your time in the womb, however, it is very helpful in your dealings with other people to realise that we also have expectations based on past life experiences. If you have had a former life as a pioneer who was not recognised and was persecuted by the establishment, it could understandably distort your view of authority in a future life. You might be rebellious and suspicious of people in authority when this feeling is totally uncalled for. If you had a bad experience with a religion in a past life, you might be against the religion you were born into in this life when this feeling is no longer appropriate. You may also carry guilt from a past life. For example, you might have been a coal mine owner in Victorian days, who was cruel and mean to your workers. You may come back in this life as a leading figure in a trade union, full of vilification against the owners, which is really a subconscious manifestation of your own shame. Most markedly, you may come back as a member of the opposite sex, still holding the sexual desires you had in your former life, and regard yourself as being gay. Some people are born in, say, a male body, but feel as if they are female. They might become a transvestite or even have a sex change operation. This is a major problem for them, but rein-carnation may help them to understand why they feel that way and realise that they are here to learn a different set of lessons as a member of the opposite sex.

Just as important, but often overlooked, is the time between your last life and this one. This is when you were waiting in other realms of existence, with people of a similar evolutionary background to yourself, to be re-born. Your higher self (or soul if you prefer) chose your parents and the exact conditions under which you were born, to learn the lessons you need. You may have had a period of preparation in the other realms, particularly if you have an important task to accomplish in this life, and that preparation will come back to you in flashes, as if from nowhere, because it has been programmed into your subconscious mind. For example, if it was your task to become an important inventor, you will know, probably from childhood, that you need to study those subjects which will enable you to do this.

In starting to uncover your past life experiences, you need to be wary of false memory syndrome. What you think was a memory may in fact be your imagination or a psychic impres-sion. Different perceptions can alter recollections, and one of the things you often need to do is balance out in this life misunderstandings from past lives. You can do this without any detailed memory, but specific recollections will some-times come to you to help you to do this and to enable you to move on. It is sometimes a process of removing past baggage so that you can see more clearly what the truth of a situation really is and always was. Discrimination is crucial, and the best advice I can give you is to keep an open mind. You will sometimes not know if you have recalled something, or whether it is just your imagination, in which case leave it on the shelf for future reference. Time, interweaved with karma, will sooner or later throw more light on it and there may come a time when you actually know. There may come a time when you remember, just in the same way as you remember what you did yesterday. Even if this never happens, if you leave yourself open you will get a general pattern of the types of experiences you have had, and how they can help you either to avoid making certain mistakes in this life, or to gain greater confidence in certain aspects of life with which you seem to have a natural familiarity.

PAST LIFE MEDITATION

- *Breathe deeply and evenly with your eyes closed for a couple of minutes, feeling a sense of peace and tranquillity.*

- *Make a gentle, mental request to your subconscious as follows: take me back in time to a life which is relevant to me now.*

- *Now visualise yourself travelling back in time by imagining yourself floating through a tunnel of light. You have become a time traveller, and the tunnel is your connection with the relevant time you need to be taken to.*

- *Now imagine you are facing a mirror. Your eyes are still closed physically, but imagine you are opening them and looking at the mirror.*

- *An image of your face may appear in the imaginary mirror, which is you in a former life. Let it come alive and watch yourself as a scene develops from that life. Leave the mirror behind and see what happens. Be sure to be in control at all times, so that you can switch the practice on and off like a tap.*

- *When you have seen enough, end the practice with some more deep, even breathing to restore control.*

Please remember that the results of this exercise may be a real memory or they may just be in your imagination. As the Keys

develop and become more advanced, you will find some practices easier than others. If you achieve no results at first with
a particular practice, do not worry, just keep an open mind. If
a life is revealed to you that contains a lesson which clearly
relates to your present situation, and as a result you realise
why certain things are happening to you now, what the
karmic lesson is, and how to deal with it, then it has been
relevant and useful. If you gain more confidence in yourself as
a result of seeing what you achieved in the past, then again it
is useful. If you are just not sure whether it is relevant or not,
put it on the shelf – one day it might suddenly fall into place.
You are moving from feeling something to actually remembering it. At first you will probably not be sure one way or the
other, but with practice there may come a time when you do
not just feel things from the past, you know them to be past
life experiences. In the meantime, do not jump to conclusions, just keep an open mind. One very good rule of thumb
is not to discuss your past life feelings or recollections with
others, whether they be about yourself or anyone else. It is
something which comes through realisation at the right time
and is best not imparted to others.

KEY 18

Out-of-Body Experiences

MARIA WAS VISITING RELATIVES in Seattle, Washington, when she had a heart attack. She was taken into hospital where she suffered another close call and had to be revived. Her social worker, Kimberley Clark, who worked at Harborview Medical Center, was surprised when Maria said: 'The strangest thing happened while the doctors and nurses were working on me. I found myself looking down from the ceiling at them working on my body'. Kimberley assumed that Maria was confused until Maria informed her that she had flown up to the third floor ledge on the northern side of the building where she spotted a tennis shoe, which she was able to describe in detail. She asked Kimberley to check whether it was really there and, if so, whether her description was accurate. Kimberley agreed and reported later that she had found a room from where she could see the ledge in question and confirmed that there was indeed a tennis shoe. She could not see it in detail, however, so she retrieved it and sure enough it fitted Maria's description, including such things as a worn place where the little toe was and a lace stuck under the heel. Kimberley regarded this as evidence that Maria had had an out-of-body experience (OBE).

This is a particularly vivid example of a fairly common experience. During my paranormal phone-ins around the country, and among the many letters I receive, there are almost always reports of OBEs. Even at small lectures, with audiences of less than a hundred, there is generally at least one person who has found themselves floating above their body one night when they went to bed. According to a MORI poll in 1998, 31 per cent of British adults believe in OBEs, and 21 per cent of those have had one. This indicates that hundreds of thousands of people in this country alone claim to have experienced this phenomenon. Twenty years before this poll was conducted, Dean Shiels, Associate Professor at the University of Wisconsin, USA, published the results of his cross-culture study of beliefs in OBEs. Having collected data from nearly 70 non-Western cultures, he found that a belief in OBEs occurred in about 95 per cent of them. With statistics like this, it is hardly a phenomenon which can be described as paranormal at all – it is, in fact, a perfectly normal occurrence. Medical situations aside, it usually happens when people are in a particularly peaceful or reflective state of consciousness, which is why meditation is crucial to understanding and/or experiencing it.

❧ ASTRAL TRAVEL

One of my favourite accounts of an OBE is one of the legends concerning St Anthony of Padua (1195–1231). Even the Roman Catholic Church, which was putting people to death for claiming less than this, and still frowns on all things occult, acknowledges this particular case because of its religious significance. St Anthony was a Portuguese Franciscan friar with a great reputation as a preacher in southern France and Italy. He is the patron saint of the poor, and is often still called upon by those who have mislaid items accidentally or been robbed for the return of their lost property. One day he was preaching in a church in Limoges when he suddenly remembered that he was supposed to be reading a lesson at another church at the other end of town. St Anthony stopped his sermon, pulled his hood over his head and knelt in silence for several minutes. During that time, monks in the other church saw him suddenly appear, read the lesson and then vanish. St Anthony then stood up in the original church and continued with his sermon. If true, this is a superb example of astral travel, which many people with two simultaneous appointments would love to be able to duplicate!

There are many other accounts of astral travel which the Vatican would not be so happy with. One exponent of this practice was the great mystic and alchemist, Count Saint Germain, regarded by some as an ascended master who could inhabit the same body, without aging, for hundreds of years. He claimed to travel astrally, even beyond this world. On one occasion he was said to have physically disappeared in front of the eyes of a maidservant of Marie Antoinette, after telling her he needed to visit the Pyramids of Giza. Another renowned mystic, Apollonius of Tyana, who lived in the first century AD and was imprisoned for his outspoken views by the Roman Emperor Domitian, was reputed to have freed himself from captivity by disappearing and travelling to another location where he reappeared. But these are feats beyond regular astral travel, in which the physical body stays in one place, as in the case of Saint Anthony, while the astral body, which is a subtle aspect of the physical body, flies off to another location.

This happens to all of us, from time to time, when we sleep. In Key Ten, I described various possible dream states, but the most significant of them all is a genuine astral experience. Around the physical body is a psychic body composed of etheric material, often termed the aura. Included in this is the astral body which can leave the physical body either when you are sleeping or, under certain conditions, when you enter some form of conscious or unconscious state of projection. One radio caller informed me that they had entered an unconscious state of projection when they were in the dental chair. They suddenly found themselves floating above the chair watching the dentist working on their own teeth. Another person told me that they climbed to the top of a hill in Cornwall, sat down and suddenly floated off across the moor and circled above their own seated body, before returning to it. These are cases of unconscious projection.

Conscious projection is something else entirely. It is deliberately induced, is not easy to bring about and should not be attempted after simply reading a book. I did not experience it that way. However, it is something which may just happen to you naturally as you progress in your meditations.

MEDITATIVE ASTRAL EXPERIENCES

- *When you go to sleep, you normally lose consciousness and enter some form of trance, which leads to the sleep state. Generally you are not aware of the moment when sleep begins. A conscious astral experience happens when you are aware.*

- *While going to sleep, try to breathe as deeply and evenly as possible and be watchful of your mental processes. Start to meditate while relaxing so that you remain aware throughout the process of going to sleep. You will note from 'A Workout for the Mind' that lower levels of brain wave activity lead to both meditation and sleep. You want to stop short of the lowest levels by remaining meditative instead of vacant as you allow drowsiness to take over.*

- *If you can maintain this while going to sleep, you may find yourself leaving the body and floating up above it, looking down on your physical body asleep.*

- *At this point, many people panic and think they might never be able to return to their body, at which point they do. Try to remain calm. If you want to return to your body you can do so at any point by making a firm mental request or saying a prayer.*

- *If you are able to stay calm, remain watchful and allow your body to float off where it will. You will usually be helped by a guide at this point (see Key Nineteen).*

- *You will either travel to another realm or to some physical place. In the latter case try to remember details about the place, which you can check later.*

- *If it is another realm, you may meet someone you have known who has died, such as a relative. Alternatively, you might enjoy a very special experience which will stay with you forever.*

- *After a very clear, astral experience, even if it is in the middle of the night, you will normally wake up as soon as you return to your body.*

➤ SPIRIT LEVELS

Astral projection is an advanced practice which should not be played around with. At its best, it is one of the most exhilarating experiences you can have; at its worst, you can end up disturbed and confused. I would never try to teach anyone to do this, but I do think that people who are already experiencing things like this, which is a considerable number, should be given sensible guidelines to follow if they want them. One of the most difficult things I have ever done in my life was to deliberately project from my body one afternoon when I was not sleepy – and I have only ever done that once. It generally happens at some stage during sleep. It may be as described above, just as you are going to sleep, in which case you will remember actually leaving the body. This is the clearest type of case. More often than this it will happen in the middle of the night as part of a dream. In fact, you can go from astral experience to subconscious dream and back again, and many accounts I received are a mixed bag of mental phenomena. Sometimes you will not remember it until the next day, but it is so vivid that you know it must have been a real experience, not an imaginary one. I remember one case of a man who dreamt that he met his mother who had recently died, and received details of names and places from her, which he had never heard before. Usually, when you do remember an astral experience, you do so in vivid detail and this man remembered the names and places mentioned by his mother when he awoke the following morning. Investigations showed that these names and places really existed, which convinced him that this was a real experience. If you are not sure whether you had an OBE or a dream, as with all mystical experiences, keep an open mind and put it on the shelf. There may come a day when you will know.

That astral projection takes place is indisputable. CIA information released under the Freedom of Information Act shows that attempts were made during the cold war, behind the Iron Curtain, to develop it and use it for spying. They called it the 'apport technique'. *The Egyptian Book of the Dead* describes in detail certain of these realms in a way that indicates that they are not so different from our own, which is also born out by many of the findings of spiritualism. Dr King, an expert astral traveller, described many parts of the other realms as being similar to our own, but more conducive to mental picturisation by the inhabitants. Near-death experiences, where people have been technically dead for short periods, usually on the operating table, and are then revived are remarkable in their uniformity. Descriptions by different people, who were not familiar with any examples of this phenomenon at all until it happened to them, agree on salient points. They generally travel through what appears to be a tunnel and are met by people, usually dressed in white, who are familiar to them, such as deceased relatives. Often they enjoy the experience so much that momentarily they do not want to come back, until they remember family or other commitments in the physical world.

If you think you have never had an OBE, it may be that you have forgotten some of the experiences that take place in your sleep. Sometimes you will note mysterious changes in people around you – perhaps they are treating you with greater respect, or they are avoiding your company for no apparent reason. This can be the result of an OBE which neither of you remember, but which has altered your relationship. If so, try meditating and see whether anything comes back to you. As Sri Patanjali wisely said, it is productive to meditate on your dreams.

KEY 19

A Good Guide Guide

IN 1978 I TRAVELLED to Australia to conduct a series of lectures, courses and broadcasts relating to UFOs, yoga and healing. One evening, I was talking to a lady about these things, when suddenly I could see, in what appeared to be my imagination, a girl standing in the corner of the room. The word 'pixie' flashed into my mind, but made no apparent sense, because she was a girl, not some kind of elf. She was dressed in a long skirt reminiscent of the 1940s and wore a hat. I did not consider myself particularly psychic at the time, though I was generally intuitive, but I realised this could be a person from the other realms. I described her in detail to the lady I had just met, and she gasped: 'Oh, that's Pixie! She was my best friend who died during the war.' I had never heard of anyone called Pixie before, and my doubts subsided with this undeniable confirmation. I felt confident – in fact, completely natural – and was able to telepathically communicate further between Pixie and her friend, who was delighted to know that Pixie was still alive, albeit in a different way, and living a peaceful existence. This turned out to be my first definite contact with a guide.

Experiences like this are ten a penny. They are happening every day all over the world and always have done. From ancestor worship to spiritualism and far more besides, there have always been mechanisms for transcending death. Some are safe, such as the controlled use of clairvoyance and clairaudience, while others can be dangerous, such as entering uncontrolled trance states and playing with the ouija board. Inducing an uncontrolled trance can lead to a loss of will, and the possibility of entering trance states involuntarily when you do not wish to. Meditation is the key to maintaining control over your psychic contacts with guides, but still entering the required state of consciousness to do so. For example, the fact that the ouija board is regarded as a game makes it dangerous, even though it can lead to very accurate results, because the players do not know the forces they might be dealing with. Meditation is a slower route to the same thing, but when you are successful you are in control of the forces you are dealing with, and you will be able to judge whether the contact you are bringing about is beneficial at all. It is not a question of whether it is possible to contact the dead, but whether it is a good thing to do so.

➤ UNFINISHED BUSINESS

For the last twenty years I have had contacts from time to time with the other side. Sometimes I will go for months without a contact; sometimes there will be more than one on a single day. Recently, the husband of a lady I know died unexpectedly. She came to see me because they had had harsh words just prior to his death and she could not feel at peace until this was resolved. You cannot always make a contact when you want to, but in this case there was no diffi- culty, because the husband was just as upset as she was and desperately wanted to make it up. I could see him clearly on his knees begging for forgiveness. I was able to help them resolve this and they both felt deeply relieved as a result. Of course, a cynic could argue that it was all wish-fulfilment, but I have enough experience of this kind of thing now to know when a contact is genuine. This kind of help is beneficial for the bereaved party here in the physical world, and very often for the departed soul as well, who may find it difficult to move on until unresolved matters are cleared up.

A vivid example of this happened to me in March 1996, when I was having lunch with a longtime friend of mine, Dave Davies, lead guitarist of the rock band The Kinks. We were in an Italian restaurant, and for some reason were at a table set for three rather than two. Suddenly I saw an image of John Lennon seated in the third chair, and Dave, who is also psychic, immediately picked up a presence. John was dressed in the uniform he wore on the Sergeant Pepper album cover, which, unbeknown to me, was the last time Dave had seen him alive – prior to that The Kinks had opened for The Beatles at the Empire Theatre in Liverpool. Dave did not see him, but could hear him telepathically, and picked up the title for a song to be called 'Unfinished Business'. We pushed the food aside, took out paper and pen, and wrote the basis of a song there and then. Subsequently Dave worked on it further, with John helping and a little input from myself. It was a three-way collaboration, as opposed to a song channelled by John through us, but it is about John's interrupted life and the things he wants to say from the other side as well as a parable for all of us individually and globally. As I write, it has just been released (November 1998) as the title track on an anthology album of Dave's work with the Kinks and his solo work. I believe John may well have influenced other musicians and bands from the other side since he passed on, whether they are aware of it or not. Guides have to work with whoever is psychic enough to work with them. John also knew that Dave would have the skill and the means to follow it through once the material was written.

When people die they are very concerned to communicate to their loved ones the fact that they are still 'alive'. They want people to know that they are still there and that there is no such thing as death for anyone. Once that major point is made there is no need, in most cases, for regular contact with the departed. Many mediums use their ability as a way of maintaining emotional relationships between people, even after death. This, I believe, can be debilitating both for the bereaved and the departed. They should be getting on with their lives here and there respectively, not holding each other back. It is particularly important for the deceased person to move on and not be held back by their loved ones, who do not wish to let them go. After all, they are really only waiting for the right time to reincarnate here again.

The most acute example of a soul not moving on is a ghost, who can hardly be described as a guide, because the very thing they need most is guidance. They are people, usually harmless, who have died but remain attached to a person or a place in the physical world, and either do not realise or refuse to accept that they have really died. They either haunt buildings or people. I remember once being asked to do an exorcism, which I must say is one of my least favourite pastimes, by the mother of a teenage girl who would not leave the house. She just refused to go out. The mother suspected that she was possessed by an evil spirit and asked me to remove it. The whole area of psychic possession is closely aligned to the field of mental illness and psychics should always be aware that so-called possessions may in fact be some form of psychological disturbance, possibly even schizophrenia. By the same token, psychotherapists would do well to work with reliable psychics, because some of their patients may be in need of the correct kind of spiritual help as well as other treatment. In the case of this girl, it was easy to see the problem. It was not an evil spirit trying to stop her going out, it was her father who had died and, in a very old-fashioned way, did not like the idea of her meeting up with boys at her age. He was emotionally possessive rather than psychically possessive and was influencing her mind not to leave the house. This was completely wrong, of course, as my guides pointed out to him in no uncertain terms. They helped him to move on, as he was meant to, and detach from his daughter and the physical world in general. The next day, the girl went out and was fine thereafter. Although I explained to the mother delicately what the real cause of her daughter's problem had been, I think she chose to believe that I had exorcised an evil spirit from her.

Other than cases of bereavement or genuine unfinished business, which can be sorted out usually in one sitting, contacts with relatives and friends just for the sake of contact should be avoided. It should be a case of live and let live. The only legitimate regular contact with the other realms is for the purpose of furthering some worthwhile work, which requires inspiration and guidance. Sometimes this will be given knowingly; sometimes it will be unseen help which just comes to you. An inspired idea pops into your head and you have no clue where it came from. It may be a guide or it may be your own higher self. In some ways, it does not really matter. The main thing is that it gets through to you.

ANGELS

Angels are back in fashion. Admittedly, medieval man's ideas on the subject are somewhat different from millennium man's ideas, but both periods are marked by a widespread belief in higher spirit beings, loosely referred to as angels. A MORI poll in 1998 revealed that almost one in ten British adults believe they have had an experience with a guardian angel. Wings, harps and bunches of grapes are no longer the staple fare of an angel – nowadays most people have different tastes in music and food anyway! Modern claims of contacts with angels have varied from figures in white robes to ordinary looking people in blue jeans. The old, stereotyped ideas of heaven and hell have been replaced by a belief in places where normal people can continue to exist as themselves. How many people do you know who would be happy in the old-fashioned idea of heaven, or who really deserve to be eternally prodded in fiery hell by demons? I cannot think of any. Here are some wonderful quotes about angels from an early Christian perspective.

- You have made humans a little less than the angels – Psalms 8: 5, *Old Testament.*

- The law was promulgated by angels – Galatians 3: 19, *New Testament.*

- The first order of the holy angels possesses above all others the characteristics of fire, and the abundant participation of divine wisdom, and the possession of the highest knowledge of the divine illuminations, and the characteristic of thrones which symbolises openness to the reception of God – Dionysius the Areopagite, from *The Celestial Hierarchies*, sixth century AD.

- Angels do not have wings as birds do, but fly many times as fast, at the same pace that human thoughts travel – Hildegard of Bingen, from *Liber Vitae Meritorum*, eleventh century AD.

- We humans have a dimness of intellectual light in our souls. But this light is at its full strength in an angel, who, as Dionysius says, is a pure and brilliant mirror – St Thomas Aquinas, from *Summa Theologiae*, thirteenth century AD.

I became disillusioned with orthodox Christianity at the age of 14, partly because I could not get an answer to the question: what exactly happens when you die? Now that I have discovered the answer to that and many other questions, I can turn back to Judaeo-Christian literature and see a lot of sense. It is paralleled in Eastern writings as well, with the Buddhist belief in devas (angelic beings) populating lokas (heavenly realms), for example. Angel is a term which is used to cover many types of spiritual being, but often people who have angelic visions are really seeing their guides.

⇾ CONTACTING GUIDES

We all have guides, whether we realise it or not. They may be deceased relatives or friends who are concerned with our welfare, or they may be people we have known in former lives who wish to help us now. If we have an important task to perform in this life, they may be people we have never known before, but who are attracted to helping us because of our work. These can become the firmest friends of all. They are not infallible, even though they can generally see a more complete picture than we can, and are nearly always more clairvoyant. Dr King, who was himself a brilliant medium, told me that a guide will use a psychic or medium who is roughly on the same level as themselves. A very advanced being would not be able to communicate directly through someone who is not spiritually advanced themselves, because of the massive gulf between them. Put simply, the medium would not be able to elevate their consciousness sufficiently to establish a rapport with such a being. I do not recommend trance mediumship as a method of communication unless, like Dr King, you are adept in the practice of yoga and can therefore control the condition fully. The best method to use is clairaudience, which is the ability to listen telepathically. This ability is not easy to develop, but with practice you may be able to do so. As always, if you are not sure of your results, do not jump to any conclusions but leave them on the shelf until a time when you might know for sure.

TELEPATHIC VOICES

- *Breathe deeply and evenly.*
- *Start to watch your thoughts as they flow in and out of the brain.*

- Make a mental request that if any guide wishes to communicate, you would be grateful if they did so now.

- Continue to watch your thoughts, but also start to listen.

- If any of the words which are floating through your mind start to have a sound quality, or even a definite accent, note them.

- A pattern may build up where one particular voice comes through with a definite intonation.

- Write down any message you get. You may get something which you can independently confirm for accuracy.

- Remain in control at all times. Do not blank out your mind, and if you start to lose consciousness, stop immediately and do some deep breathing. Remember this may be a genuine contact or just your imagination. Until you get firm evidence through the information received, do not jump to conclusions either way.

- At the end, whether you get a result or not, breathe deeply and evenly for a few moments to restore balance.

- If you think you may have received a message, send a signal of thanks and then mentally detach. You must set the parameters for this type of communication from the beginning, and not allow a guide, no matter how well meaning they are, to determine this. A good guide will appreciate this and will co-operate with you.

- You have now finished and have given a definite signal in a gracious but firm way to them.

This exercise is very difficult for most people to achieve a conclusive result from. Do not be disheartened if you are not sure or even get nothing at all. There may come a time when you do get a genuine result from it, or it may just be that the guides work in a more indirect way with you.

KEY 20

Spiritual Consciousness

ASTERN LITERATURE IS FULL of examples of higher states of consciousness entered into by yogis and their chelas (students). One of the most beautiful of these is *Paramahansa*. Yogananda's autobiographical account of cosmic consciousness; he ceased to identify with his own body and mind, and became one with the universal consciousness which pervades all life. The biggest test, though, is living in the material world after such an experience. His master, Sri Yukteswar, who had induced this state in his pupil with the touch of his hand, brought him down to earth with a bump by passing him a broom as soon as he came out of the state, and instructing him to sweep the ashram (monastery). I remember a meeting between a yogi and my own master on a mountain in Devon. The yogi said to Dr King: 'You know I have been to the Godhead.' Dr King replied: 'Did you take your hat off!' The yogi looked shocked until Dr King explained that it is wonderful to achieve a state in which you truly realise the oneness of all life, but the key is what you do with it afterwards. It is not enough to dwell on it for the rest of your life, as though it was some kind of accolade; you have been given it to use. If you realise that you are one with all things, one with the divine, the next logical step is to devote your whole life in service, which this yogi was not doing. Spiritual consciousness is not another theory; it is a practical experience with practical consequences.

⇝ CONNECTIONS

Life is a framework of connections; it is an inter-related whole. The first thing you realise as you start to enter the higher spiritual states is that all life is conscious. Some so-called primitive tribes knew this better than we do, but science is gradually re-discovering the fact. The activity of the human brain is connected by scientists to complex electromagnetic patterns. Although consciousness and how it is produced is not yet fully understood by science, these patterns of electromagnetic activity are regarded as the key to understanding the relationship between consciousness and brain function. But the electromagnetic patterns in our brains pale next to the electromagnetic patterns in the sun, which are believed to follow an underlying cycle of about 22 years. Approximately every 11 years, its north magnetic pole switches to the south, and in another 11 years switches back again. This polar reversal causes massive electro-magnetic rhythms. So why should the sun not have a consciousness much greater than ours, as early sun-worshippers from many cultures believed, and some of us still believe today? And if the sun has consciousness, why not other stars and planets?

The whole cosmos is teeming with life. I wrote the following with musician Basil Simonenko for his CD of spiritual techno music:

> *All the universe is mind*
> *The sun, the stars, the galaxies*
> *Energies through deepest space*
> *Light which fashions every atom*
> *You're living in a mindfield*

But it is one thing to realise these things at an intellectual level, and another thing entirely to know them fully from within. I freely admit that I have a long way to go in this respect. There is a massive gulf between being psychic, having out-of-body experiences, remembering past life experiences and communicating with guides, all of which I have done, and entering the highest states of spiritual consciousness in which the secrets of the universe are revealed to you first hand, which I have not. Therefore I can only give you my impressions, based on what I have gleaned from those very few masters who have entered samadhic consciousness and spoken or written about it.

⤳ GLIMPSES OF REALITY

Everything in the material world is subject to change. Even happiness, which most people cite as their main goal in life, would become dull if it were constant. It would no longer be happiness; it would just be a normal state. Like a drug, you would need a bigger and bigger fix of happiness to retain the same pleasurable state, if that was all there was to life. Happiness is an aspect of spiritual awareness, but it is an evolving happiness; it is not constant. There are people who, like cows chewing in fields, seem to be satisfied with more of the same (sorry to be rude, but I am sure you are not one of them or you would not have got this far into the book). They seem to resist questioning why they are here and where they are going. For the most part they seem to be content to survive and propagate the race so that their children can do exactly the same. I say 'seem', because my experience is that when you start talking to almost anybody, they *are* interested in their purpose for being here. They want to know more about the mystery of life, they just never felt able to say so.

Spiritual consciousness takes you to a state which is changeless, not subject to time. Although it is brought about mentally, in some ways it is not a state of mind at all; it is certainly not an emotional state. Before it comes great peace, and after it great bliss. But at the point of consciousness is complete stillness. You finally realise who you are: the divine presence within all things, the ultimate spiritual self. Whatever you focus on, you become one with. And then you move beyond oneness even, to actually being the thing you have focused upon, whether it is a blade of grass or a planet. It is complete, unbounded freedom. It is better than happiness or the ultimate high. No wonder many yogis did not want to ever leave this condition once they had entered it. They would literally spend years bathing in states of higher consciousness. They would leave their bodies in a cave or some other hidden retreat and project to a higher realm where samadhi can be enjoyed more easily than it can here. The wealthiest billionaire indulging in all the pleasures life has to offer is a prisoner in a pauper's cell compared to the states experienced by these yogis and mystics.

This is the ultimate meditative state. There is no one exercise which will bring this about, it is a result of all of them. Whichever path you choose to follow, this is where they all ultimately lead. This is Christian heaven and Buddhist nirvana. Enlightenment is when you meet your God, and find that it was your Self after all.

◆ I AM

Spiritual consciousness is a process of re-identification. All meditation practices are designed to distance yourself from the false ideas of who you are. Most people think they *are* their bodily urges or their mental impressions. Just by watching the mind, you are immediately acknowledging that you are more than your mind or you would not be able to observe it. Raja yoga is the science through which you become aware of this fact, not just as an intellectual idea, but as something you feel and eventually know inside. The following exercise, based upon raja yoga practice, is designed to bring this about.

I AM CONSCIOUSNESS

- *Breathe deeply and evenly.*

- *Gradually and gently shut out all impressions of the outside world, of your body and even of thoughts, by meditating on the words, 'I AM'.*

- *Do not qualify this in any way, just repeat mentally, with deep concentration, fairly slowly, 'I AM'.*

- *Let the mind first dwell on 'I' and then pass on to 'AM' when it has digested fully this identification with the real self.*

- *If you feel a little strange at first, this is a natural reaction from the mind which is used to ruling the roost.*

- *It can lead to a deep state of peace, inner strength and a spiritual experience when you realise that you are eternal, unchanging, divine. Allow your own consciousness to produce this realisation, rather than trying to force it.*

KEY 21

Living in the Now

IN THIS WORLD EVERYTHING boils down to what you do, not just what you say or even think. You can have the finest inspirations, and they will affect the mindfield as a whole, but in the end they have to be brought into physical manifestation. All the geniuses of history have struggled with this one thing. They had the ideas, they knew that they could work, but they had to make them happen. In this day and age, as never before, that is what really counts.

❧ ONENESS

There is a plan for the enlightenment of this world, and many are being called in different ways to play their parts. Every kind of inspirational force is being used: literature, science, music, philosophy, religion, the arts, natural healing methods, systems of yoga, prayer, even the world of finance and politics. There is a role for everyone, in fact there are many vacuums waiting to be filled. We are living at the most dangerous time in history, and yet the time with the greatest potential for positive change. Those who are inspired by the needs of this time will become engaged in one way or another in this plan. They may appear to be following much the same path as everyone else, they may do many of the same things, but their motivation will be entirely different: service to all. That is the real mark of an enlightened person – what they accomplish for the world as a whole.

The enlightened person can see the difference between just advancing themselves, and taking responsibility for the advancement of others. They want to help world culture as a whole, not just their own circle of family and friends, who are naturally important to them. They do care what is happening on the other side of the globe, and feel the need to do some-thing, anything, to contribute. There can be no higher awareness than this. You could enter the deepest and most profound states of meditation, and learn nothing greater than the fact that you are integrally responsible and connected with all life and have to do all you can to help it, whether it be human, animal or plant life; even if it be inanimate, you know that you are part of the same whole.

This approach is not easy, but it is simple. With it, every-thing falls into place. When you help others, you inevitably help yourself; and when you help yourself, you do it to help others too. Divisions disappear, selfishness is transmuted, you are living the highest and most enlightened principles, not in a meditative state necessarily, but in the now. You go within yourself, so that you can contribute more, and you contribute more so that you deserve to reach higher states within your-self. There is no conflict between the two; one process feeds off the other, like breathing in and breathing out. You cannot do either all the time; you need to refuel yourself, and then you need to use that fuel in the right way. It is a spiral of light which illuminates your path, a yin and yang of evolutionary progress.

⟩ CONSCIENCE

Guilt is a dirty word nowadays. We all object to having guilt trips laid on us because they are upsetting. The question is, why do we feel guilty in the first place? If we felt guilty about nothing, we would be completely amoral and unprincipled – or absolutely perfect which is even more questionable. There is a difference, though, between feeling a sense of responsibility and feeling guilty. The former leads to something positive, the latter often does not. A better word would be 'conscience'. A spiritually advanced person listens to their conscience, not because they feel that they should, nor because they would be guilty if they did not, but because they *want* to. The greatest acts of sacrifice have been those done in a noble cause with a sense of honour. We all know people who have made sacrifices and want everyone to know about it. But there are others who feel privileged to have made sacrifices because the cause was so worthwhile. Living in the now is acting on your conscience, without any sense of guilt, 24 hours a day.

Western religions propagate the idea that you get your just deserts in the afterlife. On their death bed, people are suddenly stricken with conscience because they are worried about what will happen to them rather than out of genuine remorse. If they do not feel it then, many of them do after they die, when they can see things in a better perspective and wish they had done this or that differently. In the East, the emphasis is far more upon consciousness. The Tibetans divide the lokas (realms) into regions of thought such as spiritually minded humans, ordinary humans, humans engaged in war and anger, animals, ghosts and so on. Their thought patterns and emotional levels will attract them to a realm which vibrates accordingly. Both approaches are true because they are inseparable. Patterns of thought sooner or later lead inevitably to patterns of behaviour. The impulse which leads us to change our thinking and behaviour is conscience. True happiness is a satisfied conscience.

ADVANCED MEDITATION

With the sole exception of the spirit within us, we are composed of energy. The physical energy in the body is reflected in the etheric energy in the aura. During the most elevated meditative states, these energies are raised through the chakras (psychic centres) to higher and higher levels. The internal mystic force called kundalini, within the spinal column, is gradually taken through each major psychic centre in turn until the full potential of each one is realised. When this has been fully controlled you become a master (a term which applies equally to both men and women) in your own right.

Most advanced metaphysical treatises stop there. They do not have a concept of anything beyond this, other than a vague idea of amalgamating with the universe. In fact, the greatest masters do not dwell permanently, even in the ultimate samadhic states of cosmic consciousness. They control them completely, and are able to bring the kundalini back down the spine again to lower centres, depending upon what they want to achieve. They maintain strict control over their breathing patterns and sexual impulses, which they convert into other dynamic forms of expression. They are remarkable people who stand out clearly from the mass of humanity for anyone with eyes to see, which sadly is not too many people. While homage is being paid to the likes of Marilyn Monroe and Elvis Presley for their abilities as entertainers, some of the greatest people in history and currently alive on earth have not even been heard of by name. And they are quite content to keep it that way as they go about their work of healing a planet. Ironically enough, if the world as a whole was ready to recognise them they would not be so badly needed.

THE RHYTHM OF LIFE

This meditation is a meditation for living. It is more than being focused on the now, because that is purely a mental process. It is actually being *in* the now, because then you are flowing with the rhythm of life. Or as I wrote with Basil Simonenko:

> *Keep yourself on a natural high*
> *Perceive this world and check out why*
> *An elemental force, cutting like a knife*
> *Through the thick and thin of the rhythm of life*
>
> *Shining stars in a universe of truth*
> *Look for the answers, demand your proof*
> *When it comes knocking on your door*
> *Then take it as read and even the score*
>
> *Make that choice from your innermost voice*
> *In a universal tongue which has to be sung*
> *From the sound of your soul to the sound of the street*
> *Loud and clear with a happening beat*
>
> *Check it out, 'cause at the end of the day*
> *There's a time to chant and a time to pray*
> *There's an elemental force cutting like a knife*
> *Through the thick and thin of the rhythm of life*

I cannot offer any particular meditation for living in the now, because it is something which just happens. It cannot really be explained; it has to be experienced. First you enter higher and higher states of consciousness, then you live them in your waking and your sleeping. However, the following meditation exercise will, I hope, act as a trigger for this process.

MOTHER EARTH MEDITATION

- *If possible, do this exercise outdoors in a place where you will be undisturbed.*

- *Breathe deeply and evenly, standing barefoot if possible on the earth, sand, grass or natural stone.*

- *Become aware that beneath your feet is a living being, without whom none of us would exist as we know it.*

- *Feel a sense of gratitude to the Mother Earth who provides for all life on Her surface.*

- *Feel a sense of communion with a being much greater than we are, who in Her own way breathes, feels and meditates.*

- *Allow yourself to merge into Her, as though you were part of Her intelligent life form.*

- *Say a prayer of thanks to Her for all she has done for you and humanity as a whole.*

A Mental Meltdown

IMUST ADMIT THAT THIS book is not 'meditation lite'. It takes the subject further than some people may want to go, in which case they do not need to venture beyond the First or Second Eyes. The Third Eye is for those looking for serious advancement; it is meditation into the light.

The three Eyes all follow the same pattern, though at different levels, and each level operates in two aspects. In fact, the whole book could be summed up as a three-stage, two-phase technique. In the First Eye, the two phases are observing and visualising. First you watch your mental processes, then you introduce one or more images into your mind. In the Second Eye, the two phases are receiving and transmitting. First you receive an impression from the mindfield around you, then you transmit an impression of your own out into the mindfield. In the Third Eye, the two phases are focusing and realising. First you determine the thing you want to know about, then you realise it. Sometimes the order of the phases will vary, and sometimes, just like in and out breaths, you are not sure which came first, but know that one leads to another and back again.

In table form, the underlying technique running through *The Meditation Plan* would be as follows:

Stages	Phase One	Phase Two
1 Keys of Imagination	Observe	Visualise
2 Keys of Intuition	Receive	Transmit
3 Keys of Inspiration	Focus	Realise

So, if it is so easy to reduce it to a simple formula like this, why leave it to the end of the book? The answer to that very fair question is that I did not want it to be just another intellectual idea. Meditation is a practical thing, it is about results. You see the sun first; later you start to realise how it shines. There is no finer traditional, yogic work on how to enter samadhi than the Aphorisms of Patanjali, and yet most people who read it do not enter samadhi. As they tread the path towards this state, they increasingly see the meaning of his succinct phrases which sum up in one or two lines a whole raft of experiences. Intellectuals who have written commentaries on them have sometimes missed the point entirely, because they have not experienced what he was talking about themselves. So the starting point in this journey, no matter how far you want to take it, must always be your own individual experience.

Meditation is a kind of mental breakdown. All the seeds of individual thought are gradually consumed in the fire of advanced consciousness, until you are left only with that which is beyond mind itself. Along the way you will realise everything there is to realise about your limitless inner potential. A point which is missed in ancient works is that you can come back from this realisation and use it in the ordinary, everyday world.

How can you be divine and yet a flawed human being at

one and the same time? Dr King gave the best answer I have ever heard to that question. He said that truth has two poles, and between them there is a point of intersection where knowledge is gleaned. He did not mean by this that you have to make some kind of compromise. He meant that you have to be able to see the two opposing aspects simultaneously to know the full truth about anything. Only meditation enables you to do this. You have a personality, desires, hopes, fears and dreams. Any teaching which encourages you to deny this fact is teaching based on suppression, and it will not work. At the same time, though, you have unbounded potential; you are perfection itself. Both aspects are true. When you can accept them both and know how they can simultaneously be true, you will also start to realise why.

Once you get used to using these exercises, you will find that your way of thinking changes. Perceptions will come to you naturally. Sometimes you will want to share these with others, sometimes you won't. Priorities will change; things which seemed like insurmountable obstacles will suddenly look petty, and issues which were of no concern to you before will start to become important to you. You will be the same person and yet you will change, at least I hope you will. That is, after all, essentially why we are all here.

In 1971, at the age of 18, I went to a lecture on yoga. I was taught a yogic method of prayer and decided to try it. The results were incredible; my whole body was tingling with sensations for hours afterwards (I did not realise then that it was in fact my aura). At four in the morning I could stand it no longer; I had to know why. I got up and walked for several miles to the home of the person who had arranged the lecture and demanded an explanation for what was happening to me. He did not appreciate being woken in the middle of the night, but could see that I was concerned so he invited me to stay. The next day he introduced me to the lecturer, John Holder, who is to this day among my closest friends. John introduced me to The Aetherius Society, which changed my life (professionally as well as spiritually!). And all because I tried one exercise one day and had an experience I could not ignore. Let me know if the same thing happens to you.

Bibliography

Anand, Margot, *The Art of Everyday Ecstasy*, Piatkus, 1998

Anderson, Ken, *Coincidences*, Blandford, 1995

Berlitz, Charles, *World Of Strange Phenomena Omnibus*, Warner Books, 1995

Besant, Annie, *The Great Plan*, Theosophical Publishing House, 1920

Danielou, Alain, *Music and the Power of Sound*, Inner Traditions International, 1995

Fox, Matthew and Sheldrake, Rupert, *The Physics of Angels*, Harper Collins, 1996

Harold, Edmund, *Crystal Healing*, The Aquarian Press, 1987

King, D.D., Th. D., George, *The Nine Freedoms*, The Aetherius Society, 1963
Personal Development Cassette lectures, The Aetherius Society, 1973

Motoyama, Dr Hiroshi, *Karma and Reincarnation*, Piatkus, 1992

Patanjali, Sri, *How to Know God*, The Vedanta Society, 1953

Ramacharaka, Yogi, *Raja Yoga*, L.N. Fowler & Co. Ltd., 1960

Sivananda, Swami, *Concentration and Meditation*, The Divine Life
    Society, 1990
Vivekananda, Swami, *Raja Yoga*, Advaita Ashrama, 1970
Yogananda, Paramahansa, *Autobiography of a Yogi*, Rider Books,
    1950

❧ OTHER BOOKS BY RICHARD LAWRENCE

Unlock Your Psychic Powers, Souvenir Press, 1993
Journey Into Supermind, Souvenir Press, 1995

Co-authored with Dr George King:
Contacts with the Gods from Space, The Aetherius Society, 1996
Realise Your Inner Potential, The Aetherius Society, 1998

Audio cassette tapes by Richard Lawrence include:
Life Beyond Death: The Facts, QED, 1998
Yoga Secrets to Enhance Life, QED, 1998
UFOs: The Psychic Dimension, QED, 1998
Realise Your Inner Potential (Workshop), QED, 1998

For further information and workshops on *The Meditation Plan*,
please contact:

The Inner Potential Centre,
36 Kelvedon Road,
London SW6 5BW
Telephone: 0171 736 4187
E-mail address: www.innerpotential.org

INDEX

title of exercises are printed in **bold**.